# A REPORT ON THE CRISIS IN THE CATHOLIC CHURCH IN THE UNITED STATES

## THE NATIONAL REVIEW BOARD FOR THE PROTECTION OF CHILDREN AND YOUNG PEOPLE

*Established by the*

United States Conference of Catholic Bishops

—ᔜ—

The Honorable Anne Burke, *Interim Board Chair*

Robert S. Bennett, *Research Committee Chair*

| | |
|---|---|
| Dr. Michael Bland | William Burleigh |
| Nicholas P. Cafardi | Jane Chiles |
| Dr. Alice Bourke Hayes | Pamela Hayes |
| The Honorable Petra Jimenez Maes | Dr. Paul McHugh |
| The Honorable Leon Panetta | Ray Siegfried II |

FEBRUARY 27, 2004

In June 2002, the full body of Catholic bishops of the United States in their General Meeting in Dallas approved the *Charter for the Protection of Children and Young People*. The *Charter* created a National Review Board, which was assigned the responsibility to commission a comprehensive study of the causes and context of the crisis of sexual abuse of minors by clergy. In preparing to commission such a study, the National Review Board has undertaken firsthand research, primarily through interviews, and has presented its findings to the United States Conference of Catholic Bishops. These findings are authorized for publication by the undersigned.

—Msgr. William P. Fay
General Secretary
USCCB

First Printing, May 2004

ISBN 1-57455-628-2

## National Review Board for the Protection of Children and Young People
### 3211 FOURTH STREET NE • WASHINGTON DC 20017-1194

February 27, 2004

Justice Anne M. Burke
Robert S. Bennett, Esq.
Michael Bland, Psy.D., D.Min.
Mr. William Burleigh
Nicholas Cafardi, Esq.
Mrs. Jane Chiles
Alice Bourke Hayes, Ph.D.
Pamela D. Hayes, Esq.
Justice Petra Jimenez Maes
Paul R. McHugh, M.D.
The Honorable Leon Panetta
Mr. Ray Siegfried II

BY HAND

Most Reverend Wilton Gregory
Bishop of Belleville
President of the United States Conference of Catholic Bishops
3211 Fourth Street, N.E.
Washington, D.C. 20017

Dear Bishop Gregory:

In accordance with our mandate under the *Charter for the Protection of Children and Young People*, the members of the National Review Board for the Protection of Children and Young People present the enclosed *Report on the Crisis in the Catholic Church in the United States*. We are grateful for having been given an opportunity to be of service to the Church.

Sincerely,

Hon. Anne M. Burke
*Interim Chair*

Dr. Michael Bland

Nicholas P. Cafardi

Dr. Alice Bourke Hayes

Dr. Paul R. McHugh

Hon. Petra Jimenez Maes

Robert S. Bennett

William R. Burleigh

Jane Chiles

Pamela D. Hayes

Hon. Leon Panetta

Ray Siegfried II

Enclosure

# Table of Contents

# A Report on the Crisis in the Catholic Church in the United States.

## I.     INTRODUCTION.

The National Review Board for the Protection of Children and Young People (the "Review Board" or "Board"), composed of lay Catholics and chartered by the United States Conference of Catholic Bishops (the "Conference" or "USCCB"), issues this Report as part of its mandate to evaluate the "causes and context" of the crisis that has beset the Catholic Church in the United States as a result of the sexual abuse of minors by some members of the Catholic clergy and the inadequate response of bishops and other Church leaders to that abuse.

The Charter for the Protection of Children and Young People (the "Charter"), which the Conference adopted in June 2002, created the Review Board and directed it to "commission a comprehensive study of the causes and context of the current crisis." In response, the Board, acting through its Research Committee, has interviewed more than eighty-five individuals in sixty separate interviews, including: cardinals, archbishops, bishops, and other Church leaders in the United States and the Vatican; priests, former priests, seminarians, and theologians; victims of clergy abuse; psychiatrists, psychologists, and other medical professionals; civil lawyers, canon lawyers, and law enforcement officials; and other knowledgeable lay people. Further, the Board has consulted numerous articles and studies written or conducted by experts in pertinent fields, as well as various public records relating to reported cases of abuse. In addition, the Board commissioned a study by the John Jay College of Criminal Justice of the City University of New York to develop empirical data on the nature and scope of the problem that precipitated the crisis.

The purpose of the Report is to share the Review Board's findings and recommendations based upon its evaluation of the current crisis. Those findings seek to describe the problem and to address two fundamental questions posed by it. First, why did individuals with a disposition to prey sexually upon minors gain admission to the priesthood? Second, how did they manage to remain in the priesthood even after allegations and evidence of such abuse became known to their bishops and other Church leaders?

Concerning the first of these questions, the Report provides the Review Board's findings with respect to the process of selecting and then forming candidates for the priesthood, with special attention to issues relating to sexual orientation, celibacy, and spiritual life. Concerning the second of these questions, the Report provides the Board's findings with respect to a number of shortcomings on the part of some bishops and Church officials, including: (i) a failure to grasp the gravity of the problem of sexual abuse of minors by priests; (ii) deficiencies in the response to victims; (iii) unwarranted presumptions in favor of accused priests; (iv) reliance on secrecy and an undue emphasis on the avoidance of scandal; (v) excessive reliance on the therapeutic model in dealing with priest offenders; (vi) undue reliance upon legal advice that placed a premium on adversarial defense tactics at the expense of concern for victims of abuse; and (vii) a failure to hold themselves and other bishops accountable for mistakes, including a failure to make use of lay consultative bodies and other governance structures.

This Report also offers the Review Board's recommendations based on those findings. These include recommendations for enhanced screening, formation, and oversight of candidates for the priesthood; for increased sensitivity in responding to allegations of abuse; for greater accountability of bishops and Church leaders; for improved interaction with civil authorities; and for greater participation by the laity in the life of the Church.

The Review Board is pleased that the bishops asked a group of lay Catholics to address these important issues. The Board also appreciates the nearly uniform cooperation it received from the bishops and other Church leaders, without which this Report would not have been possible.[1] We join Pope John Paul II in

---

[1]    Of particular note, Bishop Wilton Gregory of the Diocese of Belleville (Illinois), the current President of the Conference, has offered unflagging support to the Board and its work.

earnest prayer that from this "pain" and "sorrow" might emerge "a holier priesthood, a holier episcopate, and a holier Church."

## II.    SUMMARY.

The Review Board believes that the overwhelming majority of priests serving the Church in the United States fulfill their roles honorably and chastely. According to Church records, however, there were credible allegations that several thousand priests, comprising four percent of priests in ministry over the last half-century, committed acts of sexual abuse of minors. There appears to have been a significant surge in acts of abuse beginning in the 1960s and continuing into the mid-1980s. The fallout resulting from this epidemic of abuse and the shortcomings in the response of a number of bishops and other Church leaders to that misconduct continues to this day.

The crime of sexual abuse of minors is not a problem unique to the Catholic clergy. As Pope John Paul II stated prior to the adoption of the Charter, "Abuse of the young is a grave symptom of a crisis affecting not only the Church but society as a whole." (April 23, 2002 Address of Pope John Paul II to the United States Cardinals.) Indeed, it is a contemporary societal problem that affects numerous families and many secular organizations as well as other churches and ecclesial communities. Although some evidence suggests that the abuse epidemic afflicted

4

many institutions and organizations in our country, it is beyond the Board's mission to determine whether the problem was more pervasive among Catholic clergy than it was in other sectors of society or in the general population. Reliable statistical evidence of the sexual abuse of minors is particularly difficult to obtain because, according to experts, many if not most acts of abuse occur within families and often are not reported.

Nevertheless, the number of incidents of sexual abuse of minors by Catholic clergy, at least over the past fifty years, is significant and disturbing. This is a failing not simply on the part of the priests who sexually abused minors but also on the part of those bishops and other Church leaders who did not act effectively to preclude that abuse in the first instance or respond appropriately when it occurred. These leadership failings have been shameful to the Church as both a central institution in the lives of the faithful and a moral force in the secular world, and have aggravated the harm suffered by victims and their families. The bishops themselves recognized in the Charter that both the abuse itself and the response of some of the bishops to that abuse "caused enormous pain, anger, and confusion." The bishops acknowledged that "in the past, secrecy has created an atmosphere that has inhibited the healing process and, in some cases, enabled sexually abusive behavior to be repeated." Finally, the bishops stated, "As bishops, we acknowledge our mistakes

5

and our role in that suffering, and we apologize and take responsibility for too often failing victims and our people in the past." (Charter, Preamble.)

The bishops were right to recognize their part in the crisis and the extent and gravity of the crisis. The Review Board believes, however, that effective measures have been taken to ensure the safety of minors in the Church today. Actions taken by many, but not all, dioceses in the 1980s and early 1990s significantly reduced the number of reported incidents of abuse. More recently, in the wake of the Charter, several hundred abusers who had not yet been removed from ministry were laicized or otherwise removed from ministry over the last two years. Many bishops have met with victims and their families, even if belatedly, and have seen first-hand the horrific impact abuse can have on victims and their families. In addition, most dioceses have implemented safe-environment policies that train adults to recognize the signs of abuse and teach children to report it.

Moreover, the "zero-tolerance" policy embodied in the Essential Norms adopted in 2002 by the bishops in response to the crisis specifies that no priest who has sexually abused a minor will continue in ministry. To ensure that the zero-tolerance policy is applied consistently, bishops must consult with lay review boards in assessing allegations of sexual abuse of minors and making determinations about a priest's suitability for ministry.

The policies and procedures put in place over the last two years do not remediate, nor can they excuse, the multitude of preventable acts of abuse that preceded them. But in acknowledgment of those acts of abuse as crimes and sins lies hope for the future. That hope can be fulfilled, however, only if the bishops maintain a commitment to meaningful reforms and vigilant enforcement that outlasts the immediate crisis and becomes ingrained in the character of the Church itself.

***What is the nature of the current crisis?*** Narrowly defined, the nature of the current crisis is twofold: It consists both of the sexual abuse of minors by clergy and the failure of many Church leaders to respond appropriately to that abuse. But the crisis also has a spiritual dimension, for, as is the case with all sinful conduct, it represents a failure to comport with divine law and the teachings of the Church. Unless all aspects of the crisis are addressed forthrightly, any steps to remedy it will bear only the patina of reform and renewal.

***Why did so many priests sexually abuse minors?*** Although it is not possible to pinpoint any one "cause" of the problem of sexual abuse of minors by priests, there were two overarching contributing factors:

- Dioceses and orders did not screen candidates for the priest-hood properly. As a result, many sexually dysfunctional and immature men were admitted into seminaries and later ordained into the priesthood.

- Seminaries did not form candidates for the priesthood adequately. As a result, seminarians were not prepared for the

7

challenges of the priesthood, particularly the challenge of living a chaste, celibate life.

In addition, although neither the presence of homosexually-oriented priests nor the discipline of celibacy caused the crisis, an understanding of the crisis is not possible without reference to these issues. There are, no doubt, many outstanding priests of a homosexual orientation who live chaste, celibate lives, but any evaluation of the causes and context of the current crisis must be cognizant of the fact that more than eighty percent of the abuse at issue was of a homosexual nature. Likewise, celibacy does not cause sexual abuse; but the Church did an inadequate job both of screening out those individuals who were destined to fail in meeting the demands of the priesthood, and of forming others to meet those demands, including the rigors of a celibate life.

***Why did Church leaders respond to the problem of sexual abuse so poorly for so many years?*** Perhaps even more troubling than the criminal and sinful acts of priests who engaged in abuse of minors was the failure of some bishops to respond to the abuse in an effective manner, consistent with their positions as leaders of the flock with a duty to protect the most vulnerable among us from possible predators. Sexual abuse of minors is an evil and, as one priest told the Board, knowingly allowing evil conduct to continue is "cooperation with evil." Causes of this failure include the following:

- Bishops and other Church leaders did not understand the broad nature of the problem but treated allegations as sporadic and isolated.

- Some bishops and other Church leaders often put what they erroneously believed to be the institutional concerns of the local Church above the concerns of the universal Church. The fear of scandal caused them to practice secrecy and concealment.

- The threat of litigation caused some bishops to disregard their pastoral role and adopt an adversarial stance not worthy of the Church.

- Some bishops and other Church leaders failed to comprehend fully the extent and magnitude of the harm suffered by victims of sexual abuse by priests.

- Bishops and other Church leaders relied too heavily on psychiatrists, psychologists, and lawyers in dealing with a problem that, while it undoubtedly has psychological causes and legal implications, is at its heart a problem of faith and morality.

- Bishops and other Church leaders did not do enough in the way of "fraternal correction" to ensure that their brethren dealt with the problem in an effective manner.

- Some bishops and other Church leaders placed the interests of the accused priests above those of the victims and too often declined to hear from victims directly, relying instead on denials and assurances from those accused of abuse.

- Canon law and canonical procedures made it too difficult to remove a predator priest from ministry, and bishops did not make sufficient use of what canonical authority they did have to take action against such priests and protect the children and young people of the Church.

As a result, priests who had engaged in sexual abuse of minors were, with distressing frequency, allowed to remain where they had abused, reassigned to other parishes within the same dioceses, or allowed to live in other dioceses where they posed a further threat to children that predictably materialized into additional incidents of abuse.

The leniency afforded predator priests by some bishops may in some instances have been a misguided act of forgiveness. Nevertheless, the failure of some bishops to temper forgiveness with responsible actions to insulate minors from additional acts of abuse has seriously undermined the confidence of the laity in the leadership of the Church as a whole.

***What can we as a Church do to ensure that this never happens again?*** Ultimately, the crisis besetting the Church is not a legal crisis, a media crisis, or a personnel crisis, but a crisis of trust and faith; and it is only by the living out of their faith by bishops, priests, and the laity that the Church will be able to regain trust and fulfill its mission. By enacting the Charter and the Essential Norms, the bishops have laid a framework for restoring the trust of the laity in the Church hierarchy in the United States and ensuring the safety of minors in the Church. The Review Board's most urgent hope is that the bishops zealously enforce and adhere to the Charter and the Essential Norms, which then can serve as a beacon for the Church in other countries, for other churches and ecclesial communities, and for secular organizations.

But in order for the Church to achieve the goal set out by the bishops of "restoring the bonds of trust that unite us," more must be done, through a process that involves both transparency and substantial participation by the laity. To that end, this Report offers a number of recommendations, including the following:

- *Enhanced screening, formation, and oversight.* The Church must ensure that the men selected as candidates for the priesthood in the Catholic Church are mature, well-adjusted individuals with a clear understanding of the challenges of the priesthood, including the challenge of celibacy; that candidates undergo proper formation as seminarians to meet those challenges through a process for which responsible bishops take personal ownership; and that the seminaries themselves are capable of accomplishing this mission.

- *Increased sensitivity in responding to allegations of abuse.* Church leaders must not let concerns about the rights of accused priests, the threat of scandal, and the potential adverse consequences of litigation keep them from their primary duty when faced with allegations of abuse – seeing to the welfare of victims of abuse. More openness regarding allegations and evidence of abuse, and the response thereto, is needed. Greater sensitivity to victims also requires the avoidance of harsh litigation tactics that tend to compound the pain that already has been inflicted.

- *Greater accountability of bishops and other church leaders.* The Church must choose bishops who see themselves first and foremost as pastors; and the bishops must ensure that their brother bishops act accordingly. Diocesan and presbyteral councils should be revitalized to provide an increased measure of advice and oversight for bishops; and other mechanisms, such as strengthened metropolitans, accreditation-type visita-

11

tions of the dioceses, and lay diocesan consultative boards, should be considered as a means of providing greater accountability on the part of bishops and other Church leaders.

- *Improved interaction with civil authorities.* Dioceses and orders should report all allegations of sexual abuse to the civil authorities, regardless of the circumstances or the age or perceived credibility of the accuser, and should endeavor to resolve government investigations and civil claims on reasonable terms and in a manner that minimizes the potential intrusion of civil authorities into the governance of Church matters.

- *Meaningful participation by the Christian faithful in the Church.* The bishops and other Church leaders must listen to and be responsive to the concerns of the laity. To accomplish this, the hierarchy must act with less secrecy, more transparency, and a greater openness to the gifts that all members of the Church bring to her.

## III. BACKGROUND.

### A. The National Review Board for the Protection of Children and Young People.

In June 2002, the United States Conference of Catholic Bishops voted overwhelmingly to adopt the Charter for the Protection of Children and Young People and the "Essential Norms for Diocesan/Eparchial Policies Dealing with Allegations of Sexual Abuse of Minors by Priests, Deacons, or Other Church Personnel" (the "Essential Norms") at its semi-annual conference in Dallas. The Charter acknowledged the existence of a crisis as a result of the abuse of minors by the clergy and the response to that abuse by bishops. As part of its response to that

12

crisis, the Charter created a National Review Board for the Protection of Children and Young People.

## 1. The Membership of the Review Board and Its Mission.

The following individuals have served or are serving as members of the National Review Board:

- The Honorable Anne Burke, Interim Chair of the Board, is a Justice on the Illinois Court of Appeals.

- Robert S. Bennett, Chair of the Research Committee, is a former federal prosecutor and special counsel for the United States Senate Ethics Committee and is a partner at the law firm Skadden, Arps, Slate, Meagher & Flom, LLP, in Washington, D.C.

- Michael Bland, who holds a Doctorate in Clinical Psychology and a Doctorate in Ministry, is a licensed clinical professional counselor and clinical pastoral coordinator for Victims Assistance Ministry in the Archdiocese of Chicago. Dr. Bland is also a thriving survivor of clerical sexual abuse as a minor.

- William Burleigh is the Chairman of the Board and former Chief Executive Officer of the E.W. Scripps Company.

- Nicholas P. Cafardi is the Dean of Duquesne University Law School in Pittsburgh, Pennsylvania, and holds degrees in civil law and canon law.

- Jane Chiles is the former Executive Director of the Catholic Conference of Kentucky.

- Alice Bourke Hayes, Ph.D., is the former President of the University of San Diego and a member of the boards of several companies.

- Pamela Hayes is an attorney in private practice in New York City specializing in defense litigation and civil rights.

13

- The Honorable Frank Keating, who served as a Board member and chair from June 2002 until June 2003, is the former Governor of Oklahoma and has had a distinguished career of service in the public and private sectors.

- The Honorable Petra Jimenez Maes is the Chief Justice of the New Mexico Supreme Court.

- Paul McHugh, M.D., served as the psychiatrist-in-chief at Johns Hopkins Hospital from 1975-2001 and is currently the Distinguished Service Professor at Johns Hopkins School of Medicine and Professor at the Bloomberg School of Public Health, Johns Hopkins University.

- The Honorable Leon Panetta is a former United States Congressman and Chief of Staff for President Clinton and currently serves as the Director of the Panetta Institute for Public Policy at California State University.

- Ray Siegfried II is the Chairman of the Board of the NORDAM Group, an aviation company in Tulsa, Oklahoma.[2]

Article 9 of the Charter directs the National Review Board to perform several tasks. Among these tasks is overseeing the creation and the work of a new office within the Conference – the Office of Child and Youth Protection ("OCYP"). The Charter also requires the Board to commission two discrete studies: (i) "a comprehensive study of the causes and context of the current crisis;" and (ii) "a

---

[2]    The other members of the Review Board feel compelled to note the exemplary dedication to this task that Ray Siegfried, who is in an advanced stage of Amyotrophic Lateral Sclerosis, has exhibited during his tenure on the Board. Ray's service to the Church in what he has called the "twilight of my life" stands as a testament to him and to the Church, which brings forth so much good from so many. We are all grateful to him for his strength, integrity, and commitment.

descriptive study . . . of the nature and scope of the problem within the Catholic Church in the United States, including such data as statistics on perpetrators and victims."

Although the direct source of the Review Board's authority lies in Article 9 of the Charter, the Board's ultimate authority lies in Church law. Canon 212 of the Code of Canon Law directs not only that the Christian faithful must follow the teachings of the Church, but also that they must at times make known to Church leaders their opinion on matters which pertain to the good of the Church:

> According to the knowledge, competence, and prestige which they [the laity] possess, they have the right and even at times the duty to manifest to the sacred pastors their opinion on matters which pertain to the good of the Church and to make their opinion known to the rest of the Christian faithful, without prejudice to the integrity of faith and morals, with reverence toward their pastors, and attentive to common advantage and the dignity of persons.

(Canon 212 § 3.) It is in that spirit that the members of the National Review Board undertook this effort and in that spirit that we present this Report.

## 2.    The Purpose and Scope of This Report.

This Report is the Review Board's initial response to the Charter's request for a "comprehensive study of the causes and context of the current crisis." It provides context for the data generated by the John Jay College study and identifies issues that need to be considered in a comprehensive study of the causes of the sexual abuses that occurred. Accordingly, it examines some of the most complex and vexing questions posed by that crisis, in furtherance of the goal set forth in the Charter: That the bishops may "restore the bonds of trust that unite us" and bring about "healing and reconciliation."

To understand the purpose and scope of this Report, it is helpful to emphasize what it is not. First, this Report is not intended to address Church doctrine or to serve as a sounding board for those within the Church and outside the Church who wish to use this scandal to accomplish objectives unrelated to or tangential to the goal set forth above. The problem facing the Church was not caused by Church doctrine, and the solution does not lie in questioning doctrine. Second, this Report does not address specific instances of clerical sexual abuse or inadequate episcopal response. Although the Report may refer to particular dioceses, cases or incidents on the public record by way of illustration, it is not the purpose of the Report to determine whether an individual priest or bishop was responsible for a specific act or omission. Finally, this Report is not, and does not purport to be, a scientific exercise. With the exception of the analysis of the John Jay College study, discussed below, the Report does not rely upon the scientific method. Thus, for example, the Board has not attempted to conduct a comprehensive analysis of factors that may have made sexual abuse of minors more or less likely in a particular environment, or to develop an empirically-based profile of a typical sexual abuse offender.

### 3. The Methodology Employed by the Review Board.

In preparing the Report, the Review Board, acting through its Research Committee,[3] conducted lengthy interviews with more than eighty-five witnesses, including: (i) cardinals, archbishops, and bishops in the United States and at the Vatican[4]; (ii) diocesan officials; (iii) priests, former priests, and seminarians; (iv) victims of clergy sexual abuse; (v) experts in psychiatry, psychology, and sexual abuse; (vi) civil lawyers, canon lawyers, and law enforcement authorities; (vii) concerned lay Catholics, including Catholic thinkers and authors; and (viii) members

---

[3]    Robert S. Bennett serves as the Chair of the Research Committee. Its other members are Michael Bland, William Burleigh, Nicholas P. Cafardi, Jane Chiles, Alice Bourke Hayes, Pamela Hayes, Paul McHugh, and Leon Panetta.

[4]    A note about terminology is appropriate here. There are 177 Latin Rite dioceses in the United States and one apostolic administration, each headed by a bishop known as the ordinary. In addition, many dioceses have one or more auxiliary bishops who assist the ordinary. Certain dioceses – typically those that are larger or historically important – are known as archdioceses, and the ordinary bishops of archdioceses are known as archbishops. Each archdiocese is the "metropolitan see" of an ecclesiastical province, which is comprised of the metropolitan see and the suffragan or diocesan sees in the province. In addition, there are seventeen "eparchies" in the United States, which are the Eastern Rite equivalent of dioceses. Any generic reference in this report to "dioceses" includes dioceses, archdioceses, and eparchies. In addition, any generic reference to bishops includes bishops and archbishops, including those archbishops who also serve as cardinals. Institutes of consecrated life and societies of apostolic life are groups of men or women who typically take vows or promises of poverty, chastity, and obedience. In lay language, these institutes and societies are referred to as "religious orders." Ordained priests who belong to certain orders (such as the Franciscans or Jesuits) are subject to the direct authority not of a bishop but of a "provincial" or "superior."

of diocesan lay review boards.  A list of the individuals whom the Board formally

interviewed is provided in the Appendix to this Report.[5]

In addition to those interviews and numerous less formal discussions

with knowledgeable individuals, Board members reviewed numerous books, studies,

and articles on the subject, as well as grand jury reports and depositions and other

materials produced in the course of litigation involving various dioceses.  Although

interviewing so many men and women within the Church and outside the Church has

given the Board some understanding of the causes and context of the current crisis,

there are limits to this methodology.  This Report is not the result of a multi-year

broad-based scientific study, and the findings and recommendations addressed herein

must be viewed with that in mind.  However, the Board is confident that it has

accurately placed in context the reasons for the current crisis.

---

[5]    All interviewees were told that the Report would identify them as interviewees, but they were also told that the Report would not quote them for attribu-
tion.  Accordingly, although the Report quotes liberally from the interviews,
the Report identifies the individual who made a particular statement only
generically.  Thus, for example, if the Report attributes a particular quote to a
"bishop," then the individual who made the statement to the Board would be
one of the twenty-four bishops, archbishops, and cardinals interviewed by the
Board.  This approach resulted in great candor.  Particular quotes included in
this Report were selected not on the basis of the stature of the individual who
made the statement but because they represent the views or experiences of
many of the individuals with whom the Board spoke or because they capture
in a concise fashion the essence of one of the issues raised in the Report.

**B.     Overview of the Problem of Sexual Abuse of Minors by Priests.**

In American society as a whole, sexual abuse of minors appears to be far more widespread than earlier thought. According to some estimates, one out of every four women and one out of every seven men experienced some form of sexual abuse as minors. Most abuse occurs in families. Because there are no reliable estimates of the percentage of American adults who have engaged in sexual abuse of minors, there is no way to determine whether the percentage of priests who reportedly have engaged in such conduct is higher than the percentage in the general population or in any other segment of the population, such as teachers, coaches, and youth leaders.

It is clear that the abuse of minors is not unique to the Church. However, given the moral stature of the Church, the role of priests and bishops in providing moral leadership within the Church, and the obligations of priests and bishops to foster the spiritual and moral development of children and young people, when sexual abuse of minors occurs in the Church it is particularly abhorrent. Thus, Catholics take no solace from the fact that the sexual abuse of minors occurs outside the Church as well.

In order to determine the scope and extent of sexual abuse of minors by priests, the Conference, in consultation with the Board, commissioned the research group at John Jay College of Criminal Justice to conduct comprehensive

19

surveys of all dioceses and religious orders in the United States. Although the survey results, summarized below, are extremely helpful in understanding the causes and context of the current crisis for the Church, they cannot be relied upon to make generalizations about the Church in relation to other institutions or to society as a whole, because there are no comparative data for other elements of society.

In addition, there are at least two inherent limitations to the data collected by the researchers at John Jay College. First, some dioceses and orders may not have recorded or retained all reports of allegations of abuse during this time period. Second, the data was self-reported; no audit of the files was conducted to verify its accuracy.

Nevertheless, the Review Board believes that the results of the John Jay College study provide the most complete and reliable picture to date of the nature and scope of sexual abuse of minors by members of the Catholic clergy in the United States during the latter half of the twentieth century. The Board notes, however, that the findings and recommendations set forth in this Report are not dependent on the precise nature and extent of this abuse and therefore do not rest upon the analysis of the researchers at John Jay College alone.[6]

---

[6]    In addition, the report of John Jay College addresses only the nature of the abuse of the minor not the characteristics of the abuser, such as sexual orientation, sexual continence, religious fidelity, and the like. Only a population-based interview survey contrasting offending priests against non-
(continued...)

20

## C.     The John Jay College Study.

As noted above, the bishops, through the Charter, asked the Board to examine the causes and context of the current crisis. The Conference, through the Board, commissioned a research group at the John Jay College of Criminal Justice of the City University of New York to produce a descriptive study through a comprehensive survey of all dioceses and religious orders in the United States. These surveys requested detailed information about the number of allegations of sexual abuse of minors by priests, the nature of the alleged abuse, responses of Church leaders to allegations of abuse, and many other areas.[7] The applicable time period is 1950 to 2002. Each diocese and religious order also was directed to report the total amount of money it had paid out to victims or alleged victims of sexual abuse during this time period, including money paid for counseling and attorneys' fees.[8]

---

[6]     (...continued)
offenders can fully address these aspects of the problem. As set forth in the Recommendations, the Board urges that such a scientific study be undertaken.

[7]     The study requested data on deacons and bishops as well as priests. Any reference to the number of priests here should be read as inclusive of deacons and bishops.

[8]     John Jay College researchers were not provided with the identity of any submitting diocese or order, and their report analyzes aggregate data, not data for specific dioceses or orders. Many dioceses have published on their web sites a summary of the data that they provided to John Jay College and have discussed the survey results with parishioners. The Board supports these steps and urges other dioceses, and orders, to act likewise.

The survey results, some of which are summarized below, are extremely helpful in understanding the causes and context of the current crisis for the Church. By calling for and agreeing to participate in this scientific exercise, the bishops showed real leadership, and the Board urges leaders of other institutions to follow their lead so that our society can gain a better understanding of the nature and extent of child sexual abuse in the United States.[9]

### 1.    Summary of Survey Data.[10]

Church records indicate that 4,392 priests were accused of engaging in sexual abuse of a minor between 1950 and 2002.[11] This number represents four percent of the 109,694 priests in active ministry during that time. There were

---

[9]    Ninety-seven percent of all dioceses, representing approximately ninety-nine percent of the Catholics in the United States, completed the surveys that were sent to them. The response rate for religious orders was much lower. This diocesan response rate is high by any standard, and very high in comparison to survey studies generally. The high response rate reflects the bishops' cooperation with the work of the Review Board.

[10]    The data discussed herein were provided to the Board by John Jay College. The Board has been informed that the exact numbers included herein are subject to minor modification as John Jay College researchers finalize their report over the next few weeks.

[11]    The survey results do not include "unfounded" or withdrawn allegations of abuse, but they do include allegations of abuse that were "not substantiated" and allegations for which no investigation was conducted. Given that many individuals identifying themselves as victims did not come forward until decades after the alleged abuse, often after the accused priests had died, there is no way to substantiate many allegations.

approximately 10,667 reported minor victims of clergy sexual abuse during this period, and the Church expended more than half a billion dollars in dealing with the problem.

Eighty-one percent of the victims were male. Although more than three-quarters of the victims were of an age such that the conduct does not meet the clinical definition of pedophilia, there were substantial numbers of very young children who were victimized by priests during this time period. In addition, although many of the reported acts of sexual abuse involved fondling or unspecified abuse, there was also a very large number of allegations of more grave abuse, including acts of oral sex and intercourse.

The number of priests who engaged in sexual abuse of minors and the number of victims of that abuse changed dramatically during this time period. Although there were reported acts of sexual abuse of minors in every year, the incidence of reported abuse increased by several orders of magnitude in the 1960s and 1970s. After peaking in the 1970s, the number of incidents decreased through the 1980s and 1990s even more sharply than the incidence rate had increased in the 1960s and 1970s.

The incidence of sexual molestation of a minor under eleven years of age did not vary as greatly throughout the period as did the incidence of molestation of older children. In addition, the incidence of abuse of females did not change as

23

dramatically as did the incidence of abuse of males. There was, however, a more than six-fold increase in the number of reported acts of abuse of males aged eleven to seventeen between the 1950s and the 1970s.

Finally, the data indicate that the problem of sexual abuse of minors by priests affected all areas of the country, and not simply certain dioceses that have received sustained public scrutiny, but there was significant variation from diocese to diocese. Some dioceses, even certain large dioceses, had very few or no reported acts of sexual abuse whereas many other dioceses had twenty-five or more priests with accusations of sexual abuse of minors, and one diocese reported that 165 priests in the diocese had been accused of sexual abuse of minors.

2.      **Data Relating to Accused Priests.**

According to the survey data, four percent of priests who were in ministry between 1950 and 2002 have been accused of an act of sexual abuse of minors. The prevalence was highest among diocesan priests. There were 75,694 priests in diocesan ministry between 1950 and 2002. Of those priests, allegations of sexual abuse of minors had been made against 3,265, or 4.3%. By contrast, allegations of sexual abuse of minors had been made with regard to approximately 2.7% of the approximately 34,000 religious order priests in ministry during the time period. The remaining approximately 200 priests alleged to have sexually abused a minor during this period were "extern" priests; that is, priests resident in a diocese different from the diocese in which they had been incardinated.[12]

Fifty-six percent of the accused priests had one reported allegation levied against them. Twenty-seven percent of the priests had two or three allegations levied against them. Nearly fourteen percent had four to nine allegations levied against them. Three percent had ten or more allegations levied against them; these 149 priests with ten or more reported allegations were responsible for almost 3,000 victims, or twenty-seven percent of the allegations.

### 3.     Data Relating to Victims.

Diocesan and order records identify 10,667 reports of minor victims of sexual abuse by priests. More than ten percent of these allegations were characterized as not substantiated. In addition, for approximately twenty percent of the allegations, the priest was deceased or inactive at the time of the receipt of the allegation and typically no investigation was conducted in these circumstances.[13]

---

[12]     These numbers include allegations that were not substantiated or were not investigated. Because many victims of sexual abuse never tell anybody about the abuse, however, the actual number of priests who engaged in sexual abuse of a minor during the last half century was likely higher, not lower.

[13]     That a particular allegation was not substantiated does not mean that the allegation was false; it means only that the diocese or order could not determine whether the alleged abuse actually took place.

Eighty-one percent of the reported victims were male, and nineteen percent were female. The proportion of male to female victims changed over time. In the 1950s, approximately sixty-four percent of the victims were male. That percentage increased in the 1960s to approximately seventy-six percent and increased again in the 1970s to approximately eighty-six percent and remained at or near that percentage through the 1980s.

Approximately seventy-eight percent of the reported sexual abuse victims were between the ages of eleven to seventeen when the abuse began. Sixteen percent were between the ages of eight to ten, and slightly less than six percent were younger than eight years old. Thus, although more than three-quarters of the victims were between eleven and seventeen when the abuse began, a significant number of pre-pubescent children were victimized.[14] The number of reported victims under the age of eleven has fallen each decade since the 1960s, but the fact remains that almost two thousand young children were victimized by "pedophile priests," a number that is very troubling.

---

[14]     The crisis often has been referred to in as one of "pedophile priests," which is an inaccurate, or incomplete, appellation. The *Diagnostic and Statistical Manual of the American Psychiatric Association (IV)* classifies pedophilia as a psychiatric disorder and defines it as the sexual attraction of an adult to pre-pubescent children. According to the John Jay College researchers, although it is difficult to make generalizations about whether a particular act of sexual abuse of a minor qualifies as an act of pedophilia, and the age at which puberty begins varies for each child, molestation that begins when the child is under the age of eleven is generally accepted as indicative of pedophilia.

The majority of the victims were males between the ages of eleven and seventeen.[15] The number of reported male victims in this age group increased from 353 in the 1950s, to 1,264 in the 1960s, to a peak of 2,129 in the 1970s. The number then decreased to 1,403 in the 1980s and 363 in the 1990s. The number of girls who have been the victims of sexual abuse by priests has varied much less over time. The total number of female victims between eleven and seventeen when the abuse began peaked in the 1960s at 305 and has decreased every decade since then.

### 4.     Data Relating to the Types of Reported Abuse.

There is a tremendous range in the type of abuse reported during this time period. While all abuse is reprehensible and traumatic, the range in the type of abuse is significant. As noted above, there were 10,667 reported victimizations. Dioceses and orders were asked to indicate all of the aspects of the abuse for each victimization. Thus, a single reported victimization could involve several separate

---

[15]     Unlike sexual attraction to pre-pubescent children, sexual attraction to pubescent or post-pubescent children is not considered indicative of a psychological disorder, although acting on any such attraction is rightly treated as a crime. Those who obsessively engage in sexual abuse of post-pubescent minors may suffer from a recognized disorder, such as obsessive-compulsive disorder. In addition, certain psychiatrists or psychologists designate adult men who are sexually attracted primarily to adolescent males as being "ephebophiles." The *Diagnostic and Statistical Manual of the American Psychiatric Association (IV)* does not recognize "ephebophilia" as a distinct disorder. Ephebophilia is thus not a disorder in the technical sense, but rather a newly-coined descriptive term for homosexual attraction to adolescent males.

27

acts of abuse of varying degrees. Detailed information on the nature of the abuse was not reported for a quarter of the reported allegations. 27.3% of the accused priests were accused of performing oral sex on the victim. 25.1% of the accused priests were alleged to have been involved in acts of penile penetration or attempted penetration.

### 5. Data Relating to Responses to Allegations of Abuse.

In the majority of the reported allegations when the accused priest was still living, the diocese or religious order did take some action.[16] Nearly forty percent of the accused priests participated in a sexual offender treatment program. In very few cases, however, did the diocese or order report the allegation to civil authorities. Nevertheless, according to the data, more than one hundred priests or former priests served time in prison for conduct involving sexual abuse of a minor.

Although there has been a great deal of attention paid to certain cases in which a priest who had been accused of molesting a minor took up residence in another diocese, there appear in fact to have been relatively few such incidents. According to the survey data, approximately 143 priests were alleged to have engaged in sexual abuse of a minor in more than one diocese.

---

[16]     Approximately twenty percent of the priests were either deceased, retired, or inactive at the time of the receipt of the first allegation, and dioceses and orders could take no action in those cases.

## 6. Data Relating to Time Period of the Reported Abuse.

The survey data are consistent with statements made by clergy, lawyers, psychologists, and psychiatrists, indicating that the problem of clergy sexual abuse of minors by priests significantly increased in the 1960s, peaked in the 1970s, and decreased thereafter.

According to the survey data, 9.7% of the reported allegations of abuse began in the 1950s, 26.1% in the 1960s, 35.5% in the 1970s, 22.6% in the 1980s, and 6.2% began between 1990 and 2002. Likewise, the number of priests who were reported as having engaged in sexual abuse of minors rose steadily in the 1960s, peaked in the 1970s, and declined sharply throughout the 1980s and 1990s. Priests ordained in the early 1970s were more likely to have been accused of sexual abuse of a minor than priests ordained in any other period.

As noted above, abuse of males between the ages of eleven and seventeen is primarily responsible for the spike in the incidence rate of clergy sexual abuse between the mid-1960s and the mid-1980s. The number of male victims between the ages of eleven and seventeen increased more than six-fold from the 1950s (with 353 victims) to the 1970s (with 2,129 victims). The number of male victims under the age of eleven increased significantly as well – more than three-fold – during the same period, from 135 to 434.

29

The data appear to support the view expressed by many that the crisis has an epidemic character – exploding in the late 1960s and subsiding in the 1980s. The number of reported incidents of sexual abuse of minors by priests significantly lessened after the bishops began addressing the problem more forcefully in the late 1980s and early 1990s. It must be cautioned, however, that there typically is a long lag between the occurrence of abuse and the report of that abuse, so additional allegations of abuse during that time period will be reported in the coming years. Given, however, the amount of attention paid to this issue in the last few years, and the efforts by the dioceses to identify victims, it is likely that abuse is reported more promptly today than in the past.

### D.     Prior Efforts to Address the Problem of Sexual Abuse of Minors by Priests.

To place this crisis in perspective – and to understand why it has evoked such a passionate response from the laity – it is helpful to review the circumstances leading up to the promulgation of the Charter. Psychiatric research as early as the 1930s recognized the harm suffered by victims of child sexual abuse. In the 1960s and 1970s, states enacted laws requiring certain professionals – but typically not including clergy – to report such abuse.[17] The problem of sexual abuse of minors

-------------------

[17]     Between 1962 and 1967, every state enacted a statute requiring some form of reporting of child abuse. These statutes were generally limited, however, to non-accidental physical injury, and it was not until later that the statutes were
(continued...)

did not gain widespread visibility within American society until approximately twenty years ago.

The sexual abuse of a minor long has been characterized within the Church as both a serious canonical crime and a grievous sin. Church law historically has provided for punishment for a priest who engaged in sexual abuse of a minor. According to the Third Lateran Council in 1178, clerics who engaged in pederasty or sodomy were to be "dismissed from the clerical state or else confined to monasteries to do penance."[18] A papal decree issued in 1566 stated that any cleric guilty of crimes against nature should be "handed over to the secular authorities for punishment."[19] Both the 1917 version of the Code of Canon Law – at § 2 of Canon 2359, and the most recent version, promulgated in 1983, provide for dismissal from the

---

[17]    (...continued)
amended to encompass other forms of abuse, including sexual abuse and neglect. In addition, most child abuse statutes initially required only physicians to report suspected abuse, but states have since expanded the list of mandatory reporters to include many of the professionals who work with children, and approximately half of all states now include clergy as mandatory reporters of abuse. Nevertheless, according to one government source, many of these statutes require abuse to be reported only if it is committed by a parent or caretaker.

[18]    Pope Alexander III (1158-1181). Third Lateran Council 1179, c.11 Decretals of Gregory IX (Extravagantium Liber) X.5.31.4.

[19]    St. Pope Pius V (1566-1572). Constitution Cum Primum, April 1, 1566, § 11: Codex Iuris Canonici Fontes, ed. P. Gaspari, Vatican City (Typ. Polyglottis Vaticanis, 1923), 1:200; *idem*, constitution Horrendum, August 30, 1568: *ibid.*, 1:299.

clerical state for any cleric who committed sexual abuse of a minor. Specifically, Canon 1395 provides that any cleric who "has committed an offense against the sixth commandment of the Decalogue . . . with a minor . . . is to be punished with just penalties, not excluding dismissal from the clerical state if the case so warrants."

Nevertheless, although Canon 1389 provides for a penalty, including dismissal from office, for a Church official who with culpable negligence fails to perform an act of ecclesiastical governance, Church officials in the United States rarely enforced Canon 1395. Nor have any bishops in the United States been punished under Canon 1389 for a failure to enforce Canon 1395.

Despite this history, there was only limited awareness within the Church of the widespread nature of the problem of clerical abuse of minors until the 1980s. Indeed, the roots of public and episcopal attention to this current crisis can be traced to 1984, when the case of Father Gilbert Gauthé, a former priest of the Diocese of Lafayette (Louisiana), received widespread attention. Reports that Gauthé had abused several children gained national prominence when – foreshadowing revelations in 2002 about the Boston Archdiocese – it was revealed that diocesan officials had failed to act on numerous prior reports of abuse by the same priest. As the disquieting details of the case became known, one bishop told the Board, it "awakened the whole Church in the United States"; many bishops began to realize, he added, "It could also happen in my diocese."

Indeed, other cases of abuse did begin to surface from around the country. In response, several dioceses and the Conference began to develop guidelines for responding to allegations of abuse. Some individuals pressed for a more comprehensive and uniform approach to the problem. In 1985, three individuals who had been involved with the Gauthé case drafted a report entitled "The Problem of Sexual Molestation by Roman Catholic Clergy: Meeting the Problem in a Comprehensive and Responsible Manner." Among other things, the report presented estimates of the legal and financial liability facing dioceses in the United States as a result of sexual abuse of minors by clergy and suggested policies and procedures that dioceses or orders should follow in responding to the problem. This report, widely known after the names of the authors as the Peterson-Doyle-Mouton Report, was presented at a meeting of diocesan attorneys and executive committee members of the Conference. Although the executive committee elected not to present the report's recommendations to the full Conference, the Peterson-Doyle-Mouton Report did help shape guidelines for responding to allegations of abuse that many dioceses would later adopt. In 1988, the Conference drafted a memorandum containing a set of more comprehensive guidelines for responding to allegations of abuse that all dioceses were urged to follow until they could devise their own guidelines.

At the same time that some bishops were trying to persuade others to give the issue more attention, events in different areas of the country underscored the

33

need for action. In 1991, the first of approximately 187 lawsuits and claims were levied against the Archdiocese of Santa Fe. The lawsuits alleged acts of abuse committed by priests who were receiving treatment for psychological problems at a Jemez Springs, New Mexico, center run by a group of priests known as the Servants of the Paraclete. Several notorious abusers had undergone "treatment" at the Jemez Springs center and continued to abuse after leaving the center. For example, Father Rudolph Kos, a priest of the Diocese of Dallas, was treated at the Jemez Springs center after having been accused of sexual molestation of minors but later was allowed to return to ministry. According to published reports, Kos abused more than ten young boys before he was laicized in 1998. In 1992, scores of allegations of abuse were levied against James Porter, a former priest of the Fall River (Massachusetts) diocese who had left the priesthood almost twenty years earlier in 1973. Porter had been sent to the Jemez Springs center in 1967 but had continued to molest boys after his treatment there.

In 1992, the Conference issued a policy statement reiterating the principles outlined in the 1988 memorandum. In that policy statement, the Conference set forth what has come to be known as the "Five Principles":

- Respond promptly to all allegations of abuse where there is reasonable belief that abuse has occurred.

- If such an allegation is supported by sufficient evidence, relieve the alleged offender promptly of his ministerial duties

34

and refer him to appropriate medical evaluation and intervention.

- Comply with the obligations of civil law as regards reporting the incident and cooperating with the investigation.

- Reach out to the victims and their families and communicate our sincere commitment to their spiritual and emotional well-being.

- Within the confines of respect for privacy of the individuals involved, deal as openly as possible with members of the community.

The Five Principles were not, however, binding on any of the bishops, and only about half of all dioceses implemented a sexual abuse policy at that time. Even then, dioceses did not always follow their policies consistently. Noting this, one individual who long has been involved in this issue observed to the Board, "Good people are better than good policies." As one bishop told us, "Some chose to ignore those principles . . . as we painfully discovered in Boston and in some other places." Another bishop commented, "Some bishops went home and put [the recommendations] into effect and other bishops went home and decided . . . that their colleagues were wrong, that they could proceed with business as usual." As a result, according to one bishop, "There were just very bad decisions. I just have to say that it's clear not every bishop got it." This foot-dragging was inexcusable and, as we know now, had disastrous consequences.

That same year, the Conference formed a subcommittee to address the problem of clerical sexual abuse. The subcommittee convened a meeting of experts on the sexual abuse of minors and presented a report to the Conference at its June 1993 meeting. The report admonished the USCCB to "be aware of the urgency which accompanied [its] recommendations" because "the hierarchy's authority and credibility in the United States is eroding . . . ." Based upon the report's recommendations, the Conference then formed an "Ad Hoc Committee on Sexual Abuse."

The Ad Hoc Committee was given the following broad mandate:

> (i) to look at assisting the Conference in effectively dealing with priests who sexually abuse minors and others; (ii) to examine what the Conference can do pastorally nationwide to assist in the healing of victims and their families; (iii) to address the issue of morale of bishops and priests burdened with the terrible offenses of a few; (iv) to assist bishops in screening candidates for ministry and assessing the possibility of reassignment of clergy found guilty of sexual abuse of minors; (v) to recommend steps to safeguard against sexual abuse of minors by employees or volunteers of the Church; and (vi) to address the national problem of sexual abuse of children, coming from many directions, especially from within families.

Although this was an ambitious agenda, the Ad Hoc Committee did not have as great an impact as some of the bishops had hoped it would have. One bishop claimed that this was owing to the fact that the committee "had no teeth" and was not supported by some influential bishops, out of concern that it was an intrusion on a bishop's authority and it would increase litigation against the Church.[20]

Problems continued to fester in other dioceses. Litigation was filed against the Diocese of Bridgeport and then-Bishop Egan in 1993 alleging that the diocese had been aware of complaints against certain priests since at least 1982 but had failed to take actions to remove the priests from ministry. For example, according to published reports, a 1990 diocesan memorandum indicated that there was a "developing pattern of accusations" that Father Charles Carr had abused young boys. (Significantly, Carr had been admitted into a seminary years earlier despite the fact that a priest who had known him for years reportedly had recommended against his admission, asserting that he lacked the emotional maturity required for the priesthood.) Nevertheless, Carr was not suspended until 1995. Indeed, Carr was actually reinstated in 1999 and served as a chaplain in a nursing home until Bishop Egan's successor, Bishop Lori, removed him in December 2002 and instituted laicization proceedings. Shortly after Bishop Egan left Bridgeport and was installed as Archbishop of New York, Bishop Lori settled pending litigation against the diocese for more than $12 million.

---

[20] In addition, in the early 1990s, the Conference considered gathering data on allegations of sexual abuse of minors by clergy from all U.S. dioceses. Unfortunately, the bishops voted to discontinue the study, because diocesan attorneys advised that the results would be subject to subpoena and could be used in future litigation.

Another troubled diocese was the Archdiocese of Los Angeles. After allegations were made that Cardinal Mahony, the Archbishop of Los Angeles, had allowed numerous predator priests to remain in ministry, the Archdiocese engaged in a very public spat with law enforcement authorities who questioned his level of cooperation in the criminal investigation of sexual molestation charges. The Archdiocese resisted grand jury subpoenas seeking priest personnel files by arguing that communications between a priest and his bishop were privileged. This argument did little to enhance the reputation of the Church in the United States for transparency and cooperation.

*     *     *

As the above summary of the growing awareness of the problem between 1984 and 2002 shows, at several junctures bishops were presented with opportunities to address this problem effectively. Some took advantage of those opportunities; others did not. The failure to adopt mandatory guidelines throughout the country and recalcitrance in certain dioceses in implementing voluntary ones despite burgeoning problems set the stage for the current crisis.

### E.      Manifestation of the Problem in the Boston Archdiocese.

In early 2002 news accounts revealed that the Archdiocese of Boston had transferred a serial pedophile, Father John Geoghan, from parish to parish decades earlier, despite numerous complaints that he had molested young children.

The Archdiocese first received a complaint that Geoghan had sexually abused a boy in 1979. Additional reports came in to the Archdiocese in the 1980s and 1990s. In 1989, law enforcement officials asked one of Cardinal Law's auxiliary bishops about reports that Geoghan had molested young boys. The Archdiocese informed the law enforcement authorities that Geoghan was undergoing treatment but did not disclose prior abuse allegations that had been levied against Geoghan. Geoghan continued in various positions in the Archdiocese for another decade until he was charged with sexual molestation of a ten-year-old boy. Geoghan was not laicized until 1998.

Public scrutiny later focused on another priest in the Boston Archdiocese, Father Paul Shanley. As early as 1978, the Vatican had written to Cardinal Medeiros, then-Archbishop of Boston, expressing concern about Shanley's public statements seemingly in support of homosexual conduct with minors. Shanley was shadowed by allegations of improper sexual conduct for years, with few adverse consequences to him, and was allowed to remain in ministry, albeit often on "sick leave," until 1996. It also came out that Father Joseph Birmingham, who died in 1989, had been accused of abusing at least fifty boys over a 29-year career in the Boston Archdiocese.

When news accounts brought to light the sexual abuse of minors by these and several other priests in Boston in the 1970s, 1980s, and the early 1990s, and the ineffectual response by archdiocesan officials to that abuse, Cardinal Law,

39

who succeeded Cardinal Medeiros as Archbishop of Boston in 1984, acknowledged that he had transferred priests to new parishes after they had been accused of sexually abusing minors. Cardinal Law publicly apologized and vowed both to implement a zero-tolerance policy and to provide prosecutors with the names of all priests accused of sexually abusing minors. Throughout the year, additional problems beset the Boston Archdiocese. Finally, on December 13, 2002, Cardinal Law resigned as Archbishop of Boston. He remains a member of the College of Cardinals.[21]

The Board conducted numerous interviews with individuals familiar with the response by the Boston Archdiocese to the sexual abuse of minors by priests. Based upon those interviews, as well as contemporaneous documentation and civil deposition transcripts, the Board is deeply disturbed by the situation in Boston. The picture that emerged was that of a diocese with a cadre of predator priests and a hierarchy that simply refused to confront them and stop them.

For example, Bishop John D'Arcy, who was an auxiliary bishop of the Boston Archdiocese until 1985, wrote several letters to Cardinal Law and to other auxiliary bishops voicing concerns about predator priests being allowed to remain in parish ministry. It appears that his concerns were ignored. In a December 1984 letter

---

[21]      Cardinal Law was succeeded by Archbishop Seán O'Malley. Archbishop O'Malley immediately replaced the lawyers who had long represented the Archdiocese and promptly settled numerous cases against the Archdiocese that had been pending for years.

to Cardinal Law, Bishop D'Arcy specifically expressed alarm about the conduct of Geoghan, stating quite bluntly, "Fr. Geoghan has a history of homosexual involvement with young boys." Unfortunately, in Boston, Bishop D'Arcy appeared to be a voice in the wilderness, and shortly after he raised troubling questions about a number of priests he was asked to leave Boston and was installed as Bishop of the Diocese of South Bend-Fort Wayne (Indiana).

In the early 1990s, as the number of allegations of sexual abuse of minors by priests in the Boston Archdiocese mounted, the Archdiocese created a position specifically to deal with such allegations. The priests who held that position over the years, however, made decisions that, at least in hindsight, were overly trusting of accused priests. For example, Father John McCormack, later named Bishop of Manchester (New Hampshire), held that position in the early 1990s and had responsibility for dealing with Father Shanley. Both the Vatican and lay Catholics had raised concerns about Shanley's statements seeming to endorse sexual interaction between men and boys. Yet, the Archdiocese responded to these concerns by drawing a distinction between Shanley's statements and his conduct.

Former Archdiocesan officials have asserted that they did not know at that time that victims of abuse by Shanley had filed complaints about him with the Archdiocese years earlier. Despite these complaints, which apparently were not made available to all decisionmakers, and despite Shanley's unsettling public statements (and his refusal to affirm that he followed the teachings of the Catholic Church), Shanley was allowed to relocate to Palm Springs and was provided with a letter of introduction to the Bishop of San Bernardino stating that he was a priest "in good standing" in the Archdiocese.

Although a report issued by the Massachusetts Attorney General in July 2003 concluded that neither Cardinal Law nor any of the diocesan officials who worked with him had violated any laws, it delivered a scathing rebuke of the Cardinal and other diocesan officials. According to the report, hundreds of individuals claimed to have been victimized as minors by priests in the Boston Archdiocese in the second half of the twentieth century. Pointedly, the Attorney General's report noted that its investigation "did produce evidence that the widespread abuse of children was due to an institutional acceptance of abuse and a massive and pervasive failure of leadership." The report also stated that "Cardinal Law personally participated in decisions concerning the final disposition of clergy sexual abuse cases, including decisions on whether to permit accused priests to return to ministry duties."

F.      The Response of the Vatican to the Problem.

In April 2002, Pope John Paul II summoned cardinals from the United States and the leadership of the Conference to the Vatican to discuss the problem of sexual abuse of minors by priests in the United States. Following that meeting, the Holy Father issued a clear statement that "there is no place in the priesthood or the religious life for those who would harm the young." That statement paved the way for adoption of the Charter and the Essential Norms by the bishops in June 2002.

Prior thereto, however, the Vatican had refrained from assuming a significant role with respect to the response of the bishops in the United States to allegations of sexual abuse of minors by members of the clergy. The Vatican did not recognize the scope or gravity of the problem facing the Church in the United States despite numerous warning signs; and it rebuffed earlier attempts to reform procedures for removing predator priests.[22]

Here, too, an historical perspective is instructive. Beginning in the late 1980s, a number of influential bishops in the United States began asking the Vatican to institute an expedited administrative process for the removal of priests who had sexually abused minors. This request was due, in part, to a deficiency in the canonical system, which allowed dismissal from the clerical state as a penalty for the sexual abuse of a minor, but only after a lengthy process. That process required the participation of the victim. A number of bishops, concerned in part that victims would find it traumatizing to address their abuse in a formal proceeding, were

---

[22]    The Review Board did meet with several members of the Roman Curia at the Vatican and from those meetings it was clear that the Holy See is now devoting significant attention and resources to the current crisis in the Church in the United States. In addition, the Review Board was encouraged by the wholehearted expressions of support for the work of the Board expressed by several cardinals at the Holy See.

reluctant to ask for their assistance. In addition, the full penalty of dismissal from the clerical state could not be imposed if the priest or his advocate demonstrated that the priest had acted under some type of mental illness or psychological disturbance. Since many priests who had committed such abuses had been sent to treatment centers where various diagnoses of mental illness or psychological disturbance had been rendered, the penalty of dismissal from the clerical state, even after exhaustion of the full canonical process, was unavailable in such cases.

Moreover, once a finding of guilt in a canonical penal process had been made, a convicted priest still had a right of appeal to two higher levels of ecclesiastical tribunals (at the second instance level and at the Vatican). Under canon law, an appealed sentence automatically is suspended. As a result, a priest convicted as a sexual abuser of minors after completion of a protracted diocesan penal process would not face the imposition of any penalty until years later. During those years, he would remain a priest, although perhaps without an assignment (and often without oversight).

In addition, some diocesan lawyers advised their bishop clients not to invoke a full penal process in those cases where civil litigation was pending or likely because the record of the testimony that was required to be kept in the canonical proceeding would be subject to discovery by a civil plaintiff. Thus, some bishops may have refrained from enforcing canon law to remove predator priests out of concern that victims and their lawyers would gain access to additional information about the priests.

To allow a predator priest to remain in ministry out of fear of litigation is simply immoral. Such an action is also short-sighted as the failure to take action against a predator priest increases the long-term legal exposure of the diocese.

When bishops in the United States first requested a process to deal with sexual abuse of minors by priests, it appears that the seriousness of this issue and the magnitude of the problem were not appreciated fully in Rome, perhaps in part because, as noted above, some bishops elected to sidestep the canonical process and consequently never prosecuted cases that reached the Vatican. In any event, these requests for an expedited process were not granted, largely out of concern that such a process would prejudice the rights of the accused priests, even though the bishops who had made the request were careful to restrict it to those situations where the priest's guilt already had been established in an impartial and objective forum, such as a state criminal trial or civil litigation where the priest had been afforded full defense rights.

Requests to the Vatican by a number of bishops in the United States for an expedited dismissal process were repeated throughout the 1990s, but again to no avail. In 1993, however, Pope John Paul II sent a letter to the bishops in the United States acknowledging that the issue of sexual abuse of minors was arising frequently during their visits to the Holy See. As a result, Pope John Paul II agreed to form a joint committee of experts from the Vatican and the Conference to study how the "universal canonical norms can best be applied to the particular situation of the United States." This Committee approved experimental changes in canon law, effective as of April 1994, which included expanding the limitations period within which a laicization proceeding could be instituted against a priest under canon law on grounds of sexual abuse of a minor until the victim's twenty-eighth birthday. It was not until February 2003, however, that the Vatican created the requested expedited process for the laicization of priests who have sexually abused minors.

Many attribute the Vatican's inaction prior to the current crisis to a general reluctance to interfere with bishops.[23] Others attribute it to a view in Rome that the sexual abuse of minors by members of the Catholic clergy was uniquely an American problem. Whatever the cause of its earlier inaction, the Vatican did respond with strong statements once the depth of the scandal and full weight of its implications became apparent in 2002. After meeting with United States Cardinals in April 2002, Pope John Paul II stated that he was "deeply grieved by the fact that

---

[23]    In fact, some witnesses stated that the Vatican had not sufficiently criticized or pressured recalcitrant bishops in the United States. The Church is understandably sensitive to preserving its independence from secular authorities, which in many areas of the world still attempt to influence the selection of bishops. Nevertheless, allowing a bishop to remain in office after he, due to his own actions or omissions, has lost support from Catholics in the diocese, priests in the diocese, and other bishops erodes the authority of all bishops.

priests and religious, whose vocation it is to help people live holy lives in the sight of God, have themselves caused such suffering," and that, as a result of the inadequate response to such conduct, "the Church is viewed with distrust." A solution to the crisis must, he said, be built "upon the solid foundation of faith." These statements provided a spiritual framework for the work of the Conference in the ensuing months.[24]

### G.     The Charter and the Essential Norms.

At its meeting in Dallas in June 2002, the Conference considered a collective response to the crisis – the Charter for the Protection of Children and Young People – and a companion set of national standards for dealing with sexual abuse of minors cases – the Essential Norms, which include, among other things, a mandate that any priest who has engaged in a single act of sexual abuse of a minor be removed permanently from ministry. The Conference approved both the Charter and the Essential Norms; and, after a joint commission of bishops from the United States

---

[24]     Charges that the Vatican promulgated a policy of secrecy for dealing with allegations of sexual abuse by priests are, however, without basis. Although some have claimed that a 1962 Vatican document, known as *Crimen Sollicitationis*, instituted a policy of secrecy for cases involving clerical sexual abuse of a minor, the document clearly was intended to apply only to the limited situation of allegations that a priest had used the sacrament of reconciliation to facilitate or conceal the abuse. Because priests are prohibited from discussing anything learned in the confessional, *Crimen Sollicitationis* established special procedures for these limited instances. It appears that few, if any, U.S. bishops had even heard of the document until 2003, when it was unearthed by plaintiffs' attorneys.

and officials from the Vatican resolved perceived conflicts between the Essential Norms and canon law, the Vatican issued its *recognitio* of the Essential Norms, rendering them particular law for the dioceses and religious communities of priests located in the United States.[25]

The adoption of the Charter for the Protection of Children and Young People is a milestone in the history of the Church in America. The Charter and the Essential Norms, even with their imperfections, can serve as a blueprint for organizations dealing with this difficult issue. As a result of the implementation of the Charter and the Essential Norms, the Board is confident that effective measures are in place today to help ensure the safety of children and young people in the Church.

### 1.    The Articles of the Charter.

The Articles that comprise the Charter are divided into four sections, each dealing with a different aspect of the crisis. The first three articles are intended

---

[25]    Some commentators have charged that the revised Essential Norms were watered down by the Vatican, but the resulting changes do not in any way weaken the mandate to ensure that any priest who has engaged in an act of sexual abuse of a minor be removed permanently from ministry. Perhaps the most significant change is the imposition of a ten-year limitations period for imposing canonical penalties on a cleric. But that ten-year period does not begin to run until the victim reaches the age of majority, and the bishop must seek a waiver from the Holy See when the statute of limitations already has expired. In any event, a bishop, by virtue of his "executive power of governance," must remove a priest from ministry who has engaged in a single act of sexual abuse even if that priest is not laicized. Other changes strengthened the Essential Norms by, for example, clarifying that the Essential Norms apply with equal force to religious order priests and deacons.

48

"to promote healing and reconciliation with victims/survivors of sexual abuse of minors." Article 1 requires every diocese to work with victims and their support groups. Article 2 requires every diocese to "have a competent person or persons to coordinate assistance for the immediate pastoral care of persons who claim to have been sexually abused as minors by clergy or other Church personnel." Article 2 also requires every diocese to have a lay review board to assess allegations of sexual abuse.[26] Its procedures must be made public. Article 3 prohibits dioceses from entering into confidentiality agreements, "except for grave and substantial reasons brought forward by the victim/survivor and noted in the text of the agreement."

Articles 4 through 7 are intended "to guarantee an effective response to allegations of sexual abuse of minors." Article 4 requires dioceses to "report an allegation of sexual abuse of a person who is a minor to the public authorities" and to cooperate with civil authorities about reporting cases in which the victim is no longer a minor. Article 5 embodies the "zero-tolerance" principle of the Charter. It requires dioceses to perform "promptly" and "objectively" a preliminary investigation when any allegation of sexual abuse of a minor by a priest is received. If the investigation

---

[26]  The Review Board interviewed several members of the clergy review board in the Archdiocese of Los Angeles and the clergy review board in the Archdiocese of St. Paul-Minneapolis as well as the head of the board in the Archdiocese of Detroit. The Board was struck by the expertise and dedication of these review board members. Such review boards can serve as a model for lay involvement in important Church issues.

indicates that the priest has engaged in sexual abuse, the bishop must notify the Vatican and "relieve the alleged offender promptly of his ministerial duties." If the priest admits the charge or if the truth of the allegation is established by the investigation, the priest must be "permanently removed from ministry" and the bishop must seek laicization, unless the priest is aged or infirm. Article 6 requires dioceses to establish "clear and well-publicized . . . standards of ministerial behavior for clergy and other Church personnel." Article 7 requires dioceses to deal with allegations of sexual abuse of minors with "transparency and openness."

Articles 8 through 11 are intended "to ensure the accountability of our procedures." Article 8 calls for the creation of the Office for Child and Youth Protection and provides the mandate for this body. The OCYP is responsible, among other things, for assisting dioceses in creating "safe environment" programs and auditing all dioceses for compliance with the Charter.[27]

Article 9 directs that the Review Board shall assist and monitor the OCYP. Article 9 also provides a basis for this Report:

> To understand the problem more fully and to enhance the effective-
> ness of our future response, the National Review Board will commis-
> sion a comprehensive study of the causes and context of the current

---

[27] In January 2004, the OCYP issued its first audit report. The report stated that more than ninety percent of the dioceses were in full compliance with the Charter. The report included numerous suggestions for improving practices and recommended that the dioceses complete a second audit the following year.

crisis. The Board will also commission a descriptive study, with the full cooperation of our dioceses/eparchies, of the nature and scope of the problem within the Catholic Church in the United States, including such data as statistics on perpetrators and victims.

Article 10 requires the re-organization of the Ad Hoc Committee to ensure regional representation. Article 11 requires the President of the Conference to inform the Holy See of the manner in which the bishops are addressing the crisis.

Articles 12 through 17 are intended "to protect the faithful in the future." Article 12 directs dioceses to establish "safe environment" programs. Article 13 requires dioceses to perform background investigations on all diocesan and parish personnel who have regular contact with minors. Article 14 prohibits transferring any priest who has committed an act of sexual abuse of a minor to a new diocese or province. Article 15 directs the bishops to coordinate with leaders of religious orders in responding to allegations of sexual abuse of minors. Article 16 expresses the willingness of the bishops to coordinate with other churches, religious bodies, institutions of learning, and other interested organizations in conducting research in the area of sexual abuse of minors. Article 17 requires the bishops to offer "complete cooperation" with an upcoming Apostolic Visitation of seminaries, which "will focus on the question of human formation for celibate chastity," and requires the bishops to develop "systematic ongoing formation programs . . . to assist priests in their living out of their vocation."

51

## 2. The Essential Norms.

The Essential Norms, which apply with equal force to dioceses and to religious orders, set forth the procedures that implement the Charter's broad principles. Unlike the Articles of the Charter, the Essential Norms are Church law for the dioceses and orders located in the United States. Accordingly, violation of any of the Essential Norms carries with it canonical penalties.

The Preamble to the Essential Norms attempts to define sexual abuse of a minor:

> Sexual abuse of a minor includes sexual molestation or sexual exploitation of a minor and other behavior by which an adult uses a minor as an object of sexual gratification. Sexual abuse has been defined by different civil authorities in various ways, and these norms do not adopt any particular definition provided in civil law. Rather, the transgressions in question relate to obligations arising from divine commands regarding human sexual interaction as conveyed to us by the sixth commandment of the Decalogue. Thus, the norm to be considered in assessing an allegation of sexual abuse of a minor is whether conduct or interaction with a minor qualifies as an external, objectively grave violation of the sixth commandment . . . . A canonical offence against the sixth commandment of the Decalogue . . . need not be a complete act of intercourse. Nor, to be objectively grave, does an act need to involve force, physical contact, or a discernible harmful outcome.

This definition is expansive and somewhat amorphous. One consequence of this broad definition of sexual abuse is that all acts of improper sexual conduct with a minor are subject to the Charter's zero-tolerance policy, irrespective of the degree of impropriety or seriousness of the consequences. The drastic consequences of a

52

finding of abuse place a premium on determining in each given case whether the conduct at issue meets the definition set forth in the Essential Norms.

Many of the Essential Norms themselves essentially mirror the articles of the Charter. Thus, for example, Norm 2 requires every diocese to have a written policy on the sexual abuse of minors by priests, a copy of which is to be filed with the Conference. Norm 3 requires the designation of a victim assistance coordinator. Norm 4 requires dioceses to have a review board to review policies and cases relating to sexual abuse of minors by priests, and Norm 5 specifies the composition of the review boards, requiring that a majority of the members not be in the diocese's employ.

The Essential Norms also enumerate the procedures that must be followed when an allegation of abuse is made. Norm 6 requires the diocese to conduct a preliminary investigation "in harmony with canon law" upon receipt of an allegation. When there is "sufficient evidence that sexual abuse of a minor has occurred," the Norm requires the bishop or religious ordinary to inform the appropriate officials at the Vatican, remove the accused from sacred ministry, limit his area of residence, and prohibit his public participation in celebration of the Eucharist pending the outcome of the process. Norm 7 provides that the alleged offender may be urged to seek an appropriate medical and psychological evaluation.

Taken together, the Charter and the Essential Norms do not provide much guidance on the conduct of an investigation. They simply provide (i) that the diocese shall conduct an investigation, in accordance with canon law, upon the receipt of an allegation; (ii) that a diocesan lay review board shall "function as a confidential consultive body to the bishop" and will advise the bishop "in his assessment of allegations of sexual abuse of minors and in his determination of suitability for ministry"; and (iii) that "all appropriate steps shall be taken to protect the reputation of the accused during the investigation." Thus, there is no guidance on the appointment of an individual to investigate allegations and no requirement that a bishop or provincial provide information about all allegations to his lay review board.

The Review Board believes that best practices in this regard would include placing an accused cleric on administrative leave pending the results of an initial investigation, having a qualified independent investigator conduct the initial investigation, and providing the lay review board with the results of all such investigations. Furthermore, we understand that the final decision regarding whether to remove a priest from ministry or institute canonical proceedings against the priest must be made by the bishop or the provincial. Nevertheless, we are hopeful that there will be few situations in which the Church official disagrees with the advice of the lay review board in this regard.[28]

Norm 8 mirrors Article 5 and embodies the "zero-tolerance" provision, requiring the immediate and permanent removal from ministry of any cleric who admits or is proven to have committed an act of sexual abuse against a minor:

> When even a single act of sexual abuse by a priest or deacon is admitted or is established after an appropriate process in accord with canon law, the offending priest or deacon will be removed permanently from ecclesiastical ministry, not excluding dismissal from the clerical state, if the case so warrants.

The Norm requires a bishop to refer to the Vatican for laicization any instance of sexual abuse of a minor which occurred within the limitations period, which is within ten years after the victim of the abuse has turned eighteen.[29] For cases that fall outside that period, Norm 8.A directs that the bishop "shall apply" to the Congregation for the Doctrine of the Faith for dispensation of the statute of limitations. Thus, the Essential Norms call for laicization for any priest who has engaged in sexual

---

[28] As noted, Norm 2 requires every diocese to promulgate a written policy on the sexual abuse of minors by clergy. Most dioceses have posted their policies on their diocesan web sites. These policies often provide additional details on the procedures for investigating and processing complaints.

[29] In February 2003, the Vatican promulgated procedures whereby a priest who had engaged in sexual abuse of a minor could be involuntarily laicized without recourse to the full range of canonical procedures. These changes are separate from those imposed by the Essential Norms and, unlike the Essential Norms, are operative throughout the world, not just in the United States.

55

abuse of a minor, whether or not the limitations period has expired.[30] The one apparent exception is set forth in Norm 8.B, which indicates that laicization is not required for aged or infirm priests. Norm 8.B dictates, however, that such a priest "ought to lead a life of prayer and penance" and "will not be permitted to celebrate Mass publicly or to administer the sacraments . . . wear clerical garb, or to present himself publicly as a priest."

Norm 9 reaffirms that bishops may, by virtue of their executive power of governance and separate from the canonical process, remove an offending cleric from office, restrict his faculties, or limit his ministry:

> At all times, the diocesan bishop/eparch has the executive power of governance, through an administrative act, to remove an offending cleric from office, to remove or restrict his faculties, and to limit his exercise of priestly ministry. Because sexual abuse of a minor by a cleric is a crime in the universal law of the Church . . . and is a crime in all jurisdictions in the United States, for the sake of the common good and observing the provisions of canon law, the diocesan bishop/eparch shall exercise this power of governance to ensure that any priest who has committed even one act of sexual abuse of a minor as described above shall not continue in active ministry.

Thus, the Essential Norms require bishops and provincials to remove a priest from active ministry even if he cannot be laicized, or pending laicization.

---

[30]    It is not clear what the dioceses have done with respect to priests who left ministry years ago as a result of allegations of sexual abuse of a minor but who were never laicized. Under the Essential Norms, it would appear that bishops should seek laicization of these individuals as well.

As noted above, Article 5 and Norm 8 provide for the removal from the priesthood of any priest who has engaged in a single act of sexual abuse of a minor. This principle has been referred to by some as a policy of "zero tolerance" or a "one-strike-you're-out" standard. It was deemed necessary because some bishops and religious superiors, in their assessment of sexual abuse of minors by priests under their authority, badly underestimated the seriousness of the misconduct and harm to the victim, and allowed wrongdoers to continue in positions of ministry, from which they went on to harm other minors. To prevent any recurrence of such situations, the Charter and Essential Norms remove any further discretion on the part of bishops and religious superiors in this regard.

Accordingly, the zero-tolerance policy applies without regard to any assessment of the degree of culpability of an offending priest based upon such factors as (i) the nature of the sexual act (*e.g.*, the improper touching of a fully clothed teenager versus the sodomization of a child), (ii) the frequency of abuse (*e.g.*, an isolated event versus a protracted history), or (iii) efforts to address the problem (*e.g.*, successful treatment of a problem that had led to an act of abuse years ago versus untreated problems that manifested themselves more recently). The policy also applies with equal force to a priest who reports himself as having engaged in an act of abuse in an effort to obtain help with his problem.

Some observers – including a group of child sexual abuse experts who participated in a Vatican-sponsored Conference last April and recently issued a report entitled "Sexual Abuse in the Catholic Church: Scientific and Legal Perspectives" – have expressed concerns about the zero-tolerance principle. Both experts and Board witnesses have noted that the public may be protected more effectively if such priests remain under Church oversight rather than if they are laicized and live in the secular world without any oversight. In addition, some individuals with whom the Board spoke question whether the policy discourages self-reporting that could pre-empt further acts of abuse, and whether it is inconsistent with concepts of natural justice and canon law that are premised upon differentiation in penalties depending upon the gravity of the misconduct. Finally, given the nature of the priesthood, laicization is an extreme remedy. As one priest said to the Board, "It's like being divorced by your wife, fired from your job, and evicted from your home all at once." Accordingly, the application of a zero-tolerance policy in certain instances strikes many observers as inconsistent with Christian mercy.

The Review Board acknowledges this is a difficult issue and that the zero-tolerance policy may seem to be too blunt an instrument for universal application. Nonetheless, the Board believes that for the immediate future the zero-tolerance policy is essential to the restoration of the trust of the laity in the leadership of the Church, provided that it is appropriately applied. In assessing individual cases in order to determine whether the priest engaged in an act of sexual abuse of a minor, the bishops must consult with the diocesan lay review board, so that together they might strive for individualized justice in light of their developing experience and expertise.[31]

The Review Board also believes that any discussion of the Charter's zero-tolerance provision would be incomplete without noting that there is no equivalent policy of zero tolerance for bishops or provincials who allowed a predator priest to remain in or return to ministry despite knowledge of the risks. In fact, in the minds of some priests, the impression was created that the Dallas Charter and the Essential Norms were the bishops' attempt to deflect criticism from themselves and onto individual priests. To the extent that this impression exists, in the minds of priests or anyone else, the members of the National Review Board stress that we see this crisis as one of the episcopacy as much as it is a crisis of the priesthood. Priests, who now stand uneasily under a sword of Damocles, with their every action scrutinized, understandably may ask why the bishops do not face such consequences if

---

[31]    Applying a zero-tolerance policy does not mean, however, that the Church can simply rid itself of a priest who has engaged in sexual abuse of a minor. Both for his own good and for the good of society, a priest who has engaged in sexual abuse of a minor should be offered psychological and spiritual counseling and succor. Furthermore, dioceses and religious orders have an obligation to these individuals as long as they remain priests. (Canon 1350, § 1.) The Church cannot simply tell them to pack their bags and leave.

they fail to abide by the Charter.[32] This distinction has deteriorated the relationship between priests and bishops. Given the events of the last two years, the bishops must place priestly morale high on their agenda and must show that they are willing to accept responsibility and consequences for poor leadership decisions if the confidence of the laity in the leadership of the Church is to be restored.

## H.     Post-Charter Developments.

Subsequent to the adoption of the Charter, several grand juries in the United States investigated whether diocesan leaders had engaged in criminal acts by not responding effectively to clerical sexual abuse of minors. At least three dioceses entered into plea agreements with state authorities. Bishops have entered into plea

---

[32]     Several priests interviewed by the Board indicated that they now feel that the public looks at priests as pariahs because of the conduct of predator priests. A story one priest told to the Board about an incident that occurred on his way to his meeting with the Board is worth quoting in full.

> I arrived at the airport early this morning to fly to Washington, and near the gate, before boarding the plane, I went to the restroom. Just ahead of me was a young mother with two small boys, about four and six. The older was saying to his mother, "We're going to go into the men's room," and she said, "Okay," until she turned around to watch them go in and saw me behind them, and looked at my clerical collar, and said to her sons, "On second thought, here in the airport, you all come with me. Follow me." And against their protest took her sons with her into the ladies' room rather than watch them follow me into the men's room.

That priests have to endure the shame of such encounters speaks volumes about the failure of the Church hierarchy on this issue.

60

agreements without either the knowledge or the understanding of the Holy See, demonstrating the general lack of scrutiny of the actions of individual bishops. In other dioceses, grand juries issued reports detailing a history of widespread sexual abuse of minors by priests and ineffectual responses to that abuse by diocesan officials. Some state authorities made public dozens of previously confidential Church files. Other state authorities imposed significant state controls on the internal workings of the Church.

- ***Diocese of Rockville Centre (New York).*** On January 17, 2003, a Special Grand Jury of the Suffolk County (New York) Supreme Court issued a report of its investigation of the handling of sexual abuse allegations by the Diocese of Rockville Centre. The report detailed testimony from several priests and victims relating to approximately twenty priests in Long Island, New York, who had sexually abused minors. According to the report, many priests witnessed or knew of these acts of abuse, but none of them reported the abuse to civil authorities. Because no law in New York required priests or diocesan authorities to report rape or other acts of child sexual abuse, the grand jury did not return an indictment against the diocese.

- ***Diocese of Manchester (New Hampshire).*** On March 3, 2003, the Attorney General of New Hampshire issued a report on its investigation of the Diocese of Manchester. The report concluded that "in multiple cases the Diocese knew that a particular priest was sexually assaulting minors" and yet "the Diocese took inadequate or no action to protect these children within the parish," and that the priest "subsequently committed additional acts" of sexual abuse against children. The diocese avoided prosecution by entering into a settlement agreement in which it acknowledged that the state had evidence "likely to sustain a conviction against the Diocese for child endangerment." The diocese agreed to comply with reporting require-

61

ments more stringent than those required by law, to submit to an annual audit conducted by the state, and to disclose to the state all facts relating to the diocese's past handling of sexual abuse allegations against priests.

- *Diocese of Phoenix.* On May 3, 2003, the Diocese of Phoenix entered into a settlement agreement with the state of Arizona. As part of the agreement, then-Bishop O'Brien acknowledged "that he allowed Roman Catholic priests under his supervision to have contact with minors after becoming aware of allegations of criminal sexual misconduct" and acknowledged "transferring offending priests to situations where children could be further victimized." In exchange for not prosecuting the bishop, the diocese agreed to comprehensive oversight by the state in certain affairs of the diocese. Among other things, by the agreement, the bishop agreed to give up authority for dealing with issues that arise relating to the revision, enforcement, and application of the diocese's sexual misconduct policy. The bishop agreed to the appointment of a Youth Protection Advocate, over whom the bishop would have no authority, and agreed to give the state input into the appointment of the counsel to the Youth Protection Advocate.

- *Archdiocese of Boston.* As noted above, in July 2003, the Massachusetts Attorney General issued a report detailing the findings of a grand jury investigation of the Archdiocese of Boston. In its public report, the Attorney General stated that the Archdiocese had refused to cooperate with the investigation, forcing the Attorney General to issue fifty-three subpoenas and compel testimony from numerous archdiocesan officials. The Attorney General required the Archdiocese to agree to provide any revised policies or procedures to the state before their adoption and publication.

- *Archdiocese of Cincinnati.* In November 2003, Archbishop Pilarczyk entered a guilty plea on behalf of the Archdiocese of Cincinnati, resulting in a finding that the Archdiocese violated Ohio law in the late 1970s and early 1980s by failing to report crimes of sexual abuse of minors by priests. The plea agreement avoided the indictment of any individuals.

In addition to these government actions, there were throughout the country in 2003 several significant settlements of civil lawsuits arising from the crisis. For example, the Archdiocese of Boston settled claims relating to Father John Geoghan and other predator priests for approximately $85 million, forcing the Archdiocese to plan the closing of a significant number of parishes and to sell the Cardinal's residence. In other dioceses, multi-million dollar settlements led to the closure of some parishes and schools and threatened the viability of some of the diocesan charitable works.

These grand jury investigations and settlement agreements and the images of bishops in courtrooms and depositions are disturbing. In addition, the Board is concerned that some of these agreements give or appear to give civil authorities power to intrude into internal Church matters. In the Board's view, any agreement between a diocese and civil authorities in which the diocese gives power to the civil authorities to oversee the diocese is a troubling infringement of the First Amendment's guarantee of the free exercise of religion. Unfortunately, it was the serious failings of some bishops that caused this exercise of state authority over Church matters. Finally, to the extent that a bishop avoids consequences for himself

63

by agreeing to provisions that impose onerous financial or operational restrictions on the diocese, the Board has grave concerns about the apparent conflict of interest.[33]

## IV.     FINDINGS.

### A.     The Presence in the Priesthood of Persons Who Have Sexually Abused Minors.

Just as no one factor "causes" a priest to molest a minor, no one cause is responsible for the incidence of sexual abuse of minors by clergy generally. The debate over what caused the current crisis often has given way to a search for an easy answer that comports with the individual observer's preconceived views. As one bishop commented to the Board, "If you're conservative, homosexuality is the problem; if you're liberal, celibacy is the problem. So you tell me who you are, and I'll tell you what the problem is."

Certainly, the debate implicates important developments in both the universal Church and the Church in the United States over the past fifty years. These developments include: the significant increase in vocations in the United States in the 1940s and 1950s; the Ecumenical Council of Bishops held from 1962 to 1965 known as Vatican II; the publication of the papal encyclical *Humanae Vitae* in 1968,

---

[33]     Many dioceses are structured as a "corporation sole," whereby the bishop owns and is responsible for all of the diocesan assets. This structure may increase the risk of a conflict of interest between the bishop and his diocese.

which reaffirmed traditional Church teaching on sexual morality and artificial contraception, and the negative reaction to that encyclical by many priests and laity in the United States, fostering what is often termed the "culture of dissent" within the American Church; the exodus of almost twenty thousand men from the priesthood in the late 1960s and 1970s; and attempts to reform the priesthood and seminary formation by Pope John Paul II, culminating with the publication in 1992 of *Pastores Dabo Vobis.*

As several priests and bishops told us, discussions about the "causes" of the current crisis often are seen as an opportunity to rehash old arguments about Vatican II and the other developments summarized above. As one bishop put it, echoing the comments of the bishop quoted above, those of a "conservative bent" lay the blame for the crisis on changes made at Vatican II and the culture of dissent, whereas the "progressives" lay the blame for the crisis on the failure to implement the reforms of Vatican II. There is, he added, a "little truth" in both points of view.

Despite the predictable liberal/conservative dichotomy, however, there is a surprising amount of consensus across the "political" spectrum regarding the issues underlying the crisis. The commonality of view among the broad range of people interviewed by the Review Board, in fact, gives credibility to the conclusions that the Board members reached as a result of their investigation.

The Review Board has determined that any discussion of the "causes and context" must address certain issues relating to the selection of candidates for the priesthood and to the formation of priests, as well as special issues relating to sexual orientation, celibacy, and spiritual life. Each of these subjects is discussed below.

1. **Issues Relating to the Selection of Candidates for the Priesthood.**

In the 1992 Apostolic Exhortation *Pastores Dabo Vobis* ("I Will Give You Shepherds"; *cf.* Jer. 3:15), Pope John Paul II emphasized the importance of selecting and training young men for the priesthood.[34]

> The formation of future priests, both diocesan and religious, and lifelong assiduous care for their personal sanctification in the ministry and for the constant updating of their pastoral commitment is considered by the Church one of the most demanding and important tasks for the future of the evangelization of humanity.

(*Pastores Dabo Vobis* ¶ 2.) Since the issuance of *Pastores Dabo Vobis*, there has been a renewed emphasis on the selection and formation of young men for the priesthood. This renewed commitment is vital, for it is clear that some men became

---

[34]    As Pope John Paul II notes, the verse from Jeremiah 3:15 – "I will give you shepherds after my own heart" – stands as a promise from God that he will never leave his people without shepherds "to gather them and guide them." Of course, Jeremiah also prophesies woe to the shepherds "who lose and scatter the sheep of my pasture" and fail to take care of his flock. As the Holy Father recognizes, a Catholic priest or bishop by virtue of his role as shepherd to the People of God can bring about both great good and great harm.

priests over the last fifty years who never should have been admitted into the seminary or never should have been allowed to continue to ordination.

The archetype for such a priest is Father John Geoghan, who molested scores of young boys in the Boston area for years and who was murdered last year while serving a ten-year prison sentence. By all accounts, Geoghan was an insecure, immature, and psychologically disturbed person, and these traits were apparent to some from the outset. In a letter written by the rector of the seminary where he was studying, Geoghan was described as having a "very pronounced immaturity." Yet, he was admitted to the seminary in 1953, ordained in 1962, and allowed to serve as a priest for more than thirty years. Geoghan reportedly began abusing boys at his first parish assignment, and scores of individuals ultimately came forward alleging that Geoghan had abused them over a course of decades at several different parishes.

There appear to be several reasons why some in the Church in the past allowed young men and boys into seminaries who did not belong there. One reason may have been that seminaries simply presumed that no one afflicted with a severe sexual dysfunction would have heard the call to the priesthood in the first instance. The notion that a bishop should not make careful inquiry of a candidate for the priesthood because he should not question a calling from God is premised on a misunderstanding of the process by which the candidate and the bishop discern whether, in fact, the candidate has such a calling.[35]

Another reason for the laxity in admissions may have been that the significant increase in candidates for the priesthood in the 1950s so overwhelmed seminaries that they did not pay sufficient attention to the strengths and weaknesses of each candidate. One bishop who had served as a seminary rector told the Board that seminaries took in almost anybody who applied during the 1950s, and many of these young men were there not because they wanted to become priests but because of family pressure. Then, as vocations declined in the 1970s and 1980s and thousands of men left the priesthood to marry, the pressure to ordain a certain number of priests may have contributed to a reluctance to determine that a particular individual was not well-suited to the priesthood for psychological reasons.

The maturity of candidates for the priesthood has played a role as well. As recently as two decades ago, many candidates for priesthood had entered

---

[35]     In his 1967 encyclical letter, *Sacerdotalis Caelibatus*, Pope Paul VI emphasized this very point: "Those who are discovered to be unfit for physical, psychological or moral reasons should be quickly removed from the path to the priesthood. Let educators appreciate that this is one of their very grave duties. They must neither indulge in false hopes and dangerous illusions nor permit the candidate to nourish these hopes in any way, with resultant damage to himself or the Church. The life of the celibate priest, which engages the whole man so totally and so delicately, excludes in fact those of insufficient physical, psychic and moral qualifications. Nor should anyone pretend that grace supplies for the defects of nature in such a man." (*Sacerdotalis Caelibatus* ¶ 64.)

the seminary when only thirteen or fourteen years of age. Numerous individuals interviewed by the Board believe that these boys were denied the opportunity to develop socially and psychologically because of the closed culture of the seminary. Some of these individuals, ordained in their mid-twenties, had the emotional maturity of adolescents. This lack of "normal" psychosexual development may have hindered some of these priests from achieving a healthy celibacy and may explain why some of them sought the company of adolescent boys. The Review Board was struck by the large number of individuals who believed that many offender priests lacked emotional and psychological maturity and considered this phenomenon to be a cause of the incidence of sexual abuse of minors by clergy. The full extent to which such immaturity leads to abuse requires further study.

Most dioceses and religious orders have closed the minor seminaries in which boys began preparing for the priesthood at age thirteen or fourteen. Although there may be outstanding minor seminaries and there may be some adolescents who are ready to enter a seminary, the Board believes, as a general rule, that the increase in the average age of new seminarians over the last two decades is a positive development. At a minimum, bishops and seminary leaders must keep in mind that formation in a minor seminary has its own special considerations. Chief among these is the development of an environment where the boys and young men are able to grow not only intellectually and spiritually but also emotionally.

In the last ten to fifteen years, dioceses and seminaries increasingly have employed psychological tests and background checks to screen candidates prior to admission. Virtually all, if not all, dioceses and seminaries now screen candidates for ordination with great care. Although there is no test that will identify a pedophile or sexual predator, psychologists now have developed improved methods for discerning the presence of a psychosexual dysfunction or personality disorder and are better able to identify certain "red flags" that indicate an individual may be prone to sexually abuse a child. Such red flags include confusion about sexual orientation, narcissism, childish interests and behavior, lack of peer relationships, and extremes in sexual development. These screening procedures should help to reduce the likelihood of ordination of individuals with sexual pathologies, although the nature of such pathologies makes their discovery uncertain. The significant decrease in reported acts of sexual abuse of minors among priests ordained since 1990 may serve as some evidence that these screening procedures are generally effective.

The Review Board thus believes that bishops and other Church leaders must continue to take advantage of psychological screening and background checks in determining whether a young man is suited to the priesthood and must bring greater consistency to their utilization of these tools. To this end, the Board believes that applicants should be required to provide written statements regarding their desire to enter the priesthood; that they should be required to respond to

70

questionnaires designed to flag issues that beg further inquiry; that they should be thoroughly interviewed; that they should be required to furnish qualified references (*e.g.*, teachers, counselors, and other presumably reliable sources); and that these references should be contacted and questioned carefully about the applicant's suitability for the vocation of the priesthood.

The process must be ongoing and interactive. In that regard, one bishop told the Board that in his diocese a candidate is interviewed several times over a significant period of time, and the quality of the candidate's social interactions as viewed over time is the predominant determinant of his suitability for the priesthood. The Board believes, further, that applicants who appear unfit should be rejected regardless of extrinsic considerations; and that the results of the application process should be shared among dioceses to avoid inconsistent determinations regarding unsuitable candidates.[36]

Nevertheless, the Board believes that psychological screening is not a substitute for the exercise of good judgment by a bishop, who should get to know every potential candidate for the priesthood before the candidate is accepted into the

---

[36]    In 1999 the Conference promulgated norms for admitting to a seminary men who previously had been enrolled as seminarians elsewhere or had been members of a religious order. Consideration should be given to establishing similar standards for admitting to a seminary men who previously had been rejected for admission by another diocese or seminary.

seminary.[37] The Holy Father's words in his recent Apostolic Exhortation *Pastores Gregis (Shepherds of the Flock)* must be heeded:

> The Bishop will not fail to visit the seminary frequently . . . . A genuine personal knowledge of the candidates for the priesthood in his particular Church is indispensable for the Bishop. On the basis of these direct contacts he will ensure that the seminaries form mature and balanced personalities, men capable of establishing sound human and pastoral relationships, knowledgeable in theology, solid in the spiritual life, and in love with the Church.

(*Pastores Gregis* ¶ 48.)

### 2. Issues Relating to the Formation of Candidates for the Priesthood.

A successful priest must be well developed not only intellectually and spiritually but also emotionally and psychologically. Given the considerable demands placed upon priests, particularly by their vow of celibacy, it is vitally important that seminaries prepare candidates properly for the full range of the implications of priesthood, including its social and sexual ramifications. On the specific issue of sexual abuse of minors, a priest's formation in a seminary is key. As one witness who had been involved for many years in treatment of offender priests told the Board, "There is a very definite relationship between [a priest's] formation experience" and the possibility that the priest will sexually abuse a minor.

---

[37]     This is so not only to ensure unsuitable candidates are not admitted, but also, to avoid the unwarranted rejection of inspired candidates merely because they appear somewhat eccentric.

For many years, seminaries focused almost exclusively on intellectual preparation and neglected human formation. Moreover, in the 1970s and 1980s, some seminaries yielded to a culture of sexual permissiveness and moral relativism. Although there have been improvements in seminary conduct over the last ten years, forming priests who are fully prepared to meet the demands of the priesthood (and dismissing those seminarians judged incapable of meeting those demands) must remain a high priority. As Pope John Paul II has written, it is the bishop's responsibility to know his seminarians; the "bishop should make a point of visiting them often and in some way 'being' with them as a way of giving significant expression to his responsibility for the formation of candidates for the priesthood." (*Pastores Dabo Vobis* ¶ 65.) Sadly, according to some witnesses, not all bishops in the United States fulfilled this responsibility.

*Pastores Dabo Vobis* states that "human formation" is the "basis of all priestly formation." Through the process of human formation, a future priest must "cultivate a series of human qualities" so that his "human personality . . . becomes a bridge and not an obstacle for others in their meeting with Jesus Christ the Redeemer of humanity." (*Pastores Dabo Vobis* ¶ 43.) Thus, seminarians "need to be educated to love the truth, to be loyal, to respect every person, to have a sense of justice, to be true to their word, to be genuinely compassionate, to be men of integrity and, especially, to be balanced in judgment and behavior." (*Id.*)

The Review Board believes that, historically, seminaries paid inadequate attention to the human formation of candidates for the priesthood. The seminary experience of the 1940s and 1950s differed radically from the seminary experience of the 1970s and 1980s, but neither was fully satisfactory. Each period had its own weaknesses that contributed to the problem. According to many witnesses, these historical problems largely have been dealt with, but much room for improvement remains.

Older members of the clergy who went through the seminary before Vatican II described an experience that focused almost exclusively on intellectual and theological formation. It was, according to one bishop, "a little bit like kind of a military academy." There was "nothing in the formation program to deal with what we now call human formation." Sexuality was not meaningfully discussed. As two bishops recounted, issues relating to the Sixth Commandment were addressed in Latin, whereas other subjects were covered in English. A third bishop echoed this and noted, "When I was in the seminary the boundary issues were taught with one sentence, 'numquam solus cum sola,' never one man [alone] with one woman. That was it."

According to numerous interviews, although some seminaries provided instruction on the Church's teachings on sexuality prior to Vatican II, they did not permit or encourage seminarians to discuss their concerns about sexuality and

74

celibacy; nor were seminarians given access to psychological counseling. As a consequence, the Board was told, some seminarians avoided or repressed their sexual problems. For some priests, it was not until well after ordination that these problems manifested themselves, often with tragic results for victims of sexual abuse.

After Vatican II and the upheaval of *Humanae Vitae* and the response to it, seminaries changed in significant ways. Some of the changes were for the better. For example, psychological and sexual issues were more freely aired, which may have reduced the risk of an unhealthy burying of sexual problems by candidates. On the other hand, some of the changes appear to have contributed to the current crisis. A large number of witnesses, both "liberal" and "conservative," agreed with the sentiment of one bishop who stated that, from the mid-1960s to the early 1980s, "seminaries lost their way." The rigid moral absolutism that had guided clergy and laity alike was giving way to moral relativism, with its attendant uncertainties and ambiguities. This may have contributed to a sense that individuals were free to do as they wished. As one bishop observed: "I think a lot of guys just lost a sense of direction, a sense of moral focus. . . . All the values that used to help them keep that dark, unredeemed side under control were just gone, and I think we just had a lot of people who let go."

It seems to be generally agreed that seminaries did not adequately address the sexual revolution that began in the 1960s, resulting in confusion about

priestly identity on the part of some seminarians and priests. One of the consequences of this confusion in identity was confusion in behavior. Many seminaries
provided seminarians with an inadequate training in the theology of the priesthood
and failed to follow Church teaching on issues of sexual morality. In some instances,
according to one bishop, the "culture of 'if it feels good, it's all right' infiltrated
seminaries" and thereby "had its infiltration in the Church." As a result, a homo-
erotic culture took root at some seminaries. The Board was told that some seminarians were propositioned (or worse) by older seminarians or faculty, and little was
done when complaints were made about this misconduct.

In addition, in the 1960s and 1970s, there was an expectation among
many that the Vatican was contemplating modifying Church doctrine on sexuality
and perhaps even abolishing the discipline of celibacy for priests. As one bishop
stated when discussing seminaries of the late 1960s and 1970s, "You had professors
who were saying, 'Don't worry; they're going to change the celibacy rule any day, and
you will be able to get married.' So guys were going through thinking that they . . .
could get married after ordination."

The Church has an obligation to ensure that its candidates for the
priesthood are made aware not only of Church doctrine and discipline, but also of the

rationale for Church doctrine and discipline.[38] The post-Vatican II obsession with psychology at many seminaries left many priests without an adequate understanding of the theological and historical basis for celibacy. The failure to have seminarians study and discuss the meaning of celibacy and the rationales for celibacy contributed to an atmosphere in which it was possible for many priests to disregard or distort their promise of celibacy. Also, "There wasn't enough attention to the spiritual life," according to one former seminary rector. He went on, "There were seminaries in which daily mass was not required, seminaries in which the divine office was not required. . . . The spiritual direction was just many times a hodgepodge."

Although some witnesses told the Board that pre-Vatican II "repression" led to problems and others told the Board that post-Vatican II laxity led to problems, all agreed that the rapidly changing climate – from a strictly regimented atmosphere to an "anything-goes" atmosphere – contributed to the current crisis. One bishop who was in the seminary during the early 1970s noted that it "was a time of transition from the old formation system to a new formation system and a lot of confusion in between – theological confusion, doctrinal confusion." But the inclination of some to "blame" Vatican II for the subsequent decline in moral standards in

---

[38] The discipline of celibacy is not mandated by Church dogma, although it has been a constant discipline in the Latin Rite Church since the twelfth century. There have been and are married priests in the Church, including priests of the Eastern Rite and priests who have converted from other churches and ecclesial communities.

the Church is simply an "easy out," as one bishop put it, that fails to take account of numerous other important factors and changes in society. The apparent significant increase in acts of sexual abuse of minors by priests in the 1960s and 1970s cannot be viewed without acknowledging significant changes in sexual behavior in the culture at large during the same time period.

Problems with seminaries in the post-Vatican II era were dealt with to a certain extent by an Apostolic Visitation of seminaries in the 1980s. This process was begun after many had expressed concerns about the direction of seminaries in the United States. The Visitation took seven years to conclude and consisted, in effect, of an accreditation-type examination of seminaries by bishops and seminary rectors. In the wake of the Apostolic Visitation, according to several observers, seminaries improved, but problems relating to acceptable standards of behavior and formation remained at some seminaries.

The Review Board believes that seminaries must deal with issues of sexual conduct more openly and more forthrightly. As *Pastores Dabo Vobis* makes clear, in current Western culture, "an education for sexuality becomes more difficult but also more urgent." (*Pastores Dabo Vobis* ¶ 44.) Even apart from the teaching of the Church on sexuality, candidates for the priesthood must be made more mindful of the criminal nature of sexual abuse of minors; they must have reinforced for them the gravity of this sin and its consequences for the victim, the priest, and the Church; and they must be encouraged to raise concerns that they have about the sexual conduct of other priests or seminarians, with the assurance that those concerns will be acted upon.

*Pastores Dabo Vobis* also stresses the importance of ongoing formation after a priest's ordination. As noted above, the Review Board believes that it is vitally important for a priest to have strong connections with others, including his bishop. Some bishops have had insufficient contact with individuals studying to be ordained in their dioceses and little contact thereafter. A bishop who does not get to know his priests and his seminarians will not be able to determine whether a person is and continues to be suited for the priesthood or is in need of counseling or other forms of assistance. In large dioceses, in particular, it appears that some bishops, who often came from other dioceses, were not able to establish and maintain sufficient contact with those under their supervision and tutelage to detect problems in their incipiency and address them in a proper manner.

*    *    *

In sum, the bishops cannot keep the promise of the Charter without continuing to reform and renew the seminaries. This reform, whether it be through the upcoming Apostolic Visitation referenced in Article 17 of the Charter or an ongoing accreditation process, must be undertaken by strong Church leaders – lay and clerical – and must include those who are not part of the current seminary system. The scrutiny must have consequences. Ridding the Church of the hundreds of priests who have engaged in sexual abuse of minors is not enough. There also must be consequences for bishops, diocesan leaders, and seminary administrators.

**3.      Special Issues Relating to Sexual Orientation.**

As noted above, the overwhelming majority of reported acts of sexual abuse of minors by members of the clergy victimized boys. Accordingly, the current crisis cannot be addressed without consideration of issues relating to homosexuality.

According to Church doctrine, homosexuality is an intrinsic disorder and homosexual acts are gravely immoral. At the same time, the Church has long been known for its position that a homosexual is not to blame for his orientation. So too, the Review Board draws a distinction between homosexual individuals and homosexual acts. We do not seek to place the blame for the sexual abuse crisis on the presence of homosexual individuals in the priesthood as there are many chaste and holy homosexual priests who are faithful to their vows of celibacy. However, we must call attention to the homosexual behavior that characterized the vast majority of the cases of abuse observed in recent decades. That eighty-one percent of the reported victims of child sexual abuse by Catholic clergy were boys shows that the crisis was characterized by homosexual behavior.

It has been reported to the Review Board that, in some areas, the large number of homosexual priests or candidates had the effect of discouraging heterosex-

80

ual men from seeking to enter the priesthood. In the 1970s and 1980s, in particular, there developed at certain seminaries a "gay subculture," and at these seminaries, according to several witnesses, homosexual liaisons occurred among students or between students and teachers. Such subcultures existed or exist in certain dioceses or orders as well. The Board believes that the failure to take disciplinary action against such conduct contributed to an atmosphere in which sexual abuse of adolescent boys by priests was more likely. In light of this background, it is vital that bishops, provincials, and seminary rectors ensure that seminaries create a climate and a culture conducive to chastity.

Before the 1990s, candidates for the seminary were not asked about their sexual orientation. Over the last fifteen years, however, as dioceses and seminaries established screening procedures, it has become routine to inquire about a candidate's sexual orientation. Currently, some bishops do not accept men with a homosexual orientation as candidates for the priesthood. Homosexual orientation is seen by some as a barrier to ordination for theological reasons, given that a priest conceptually is a generative "father" married to the Church as bride. As one bishop said to the Board: "I do believe that a priest must be able to relate to a parish the way a healthy father of a family would relate to a family . . . . It's not for nothing they call you 'Father.'" Others express a concern that individuals of a homosexual orientation face greater temptations in the priesthood or note that a homosexually-oriented candidate, unlike a heterosexually-oriented candidate, is not sacrificing the good of married life and fatherhood when he enters the priesthood.

Some of those bishops who oppose admitting homosexual candidates into the seminary acknowledge that "there are some very fine people who have been priests and religious who have been of a homosexual orientation and have done a wonderful job." Nevertheless, given what they view as the "glorification" of homosexual behavior in contemporary culture, they see too great a risk in today's climate in ordaining homosexuals to the priesthood.

Other bishops apply no such blanket prohibition and distinguish between candidates of a homosexual orientation and those who have led a "gay lifestyle." One priest who has serious concerns about the "gay subculture" in some dioceses nonetheless opposes a blanket prohibition of ordination of individuals of a homosexual orientation in the belief that ordination can be "an invitation to holiness." Moreover, "making an official declaration that homosexuals are not welcome" will not have the effect of excluding homosexuals from seminaries, religious communities, or the priesthood; but rather, "it will have the effect of driving them underground, so that this subculture exists in an even more hidden way." Even bishops who believe individuals of a homosexual orientation should be allowed to become priests stress, however, that it is the role of the priest – heterosexual or homosexual – to act as a married man because he is, according to Scripture, espoused to the Church.

Such decisions are the prerogative of a bishop, although it seems clear to the Board that the paramount question in this area must be whether a candidate for priesthood is capable of living a chaste, celibate life, not what that candidate's sexual orientation might be. But given the nature of the problem of clergy sexual abuse of minors, the realities of the culture today, and the male-oriented atmosphere of the seminary, a more searching inquiry is necessary for a homosexually-oriented man by those who decide whether he is suitable for the seminary and for ministry. For those bishops who choose to ordain homosexuals there appears to be a need for additional scrutiny and perhaps additional or specialized formation to help them with the challenge of chaste celibacy. One bishop pointedly stated that "training for celibacy is different if someone is homosexually oriented or heterosexually oriented. The occasions of sin are different. The danger flags are different."

### 4. Special Issues Relating to Celibacy.

Although the discipline of celibacy is not itself a cause of the current crisis, a failure properly to explain celibacy and prepare seminarians for a celibate life has contributed to it. As both bishops and priests made clear to the Review Board, a successful celibate life requires proper formation and discipline, without which those candidates who were most troubled sexually were most likely to fail.

According to some witnesses, certain sexually immature or conflicted individuals and certain homosexual men appear to have been attracted to the priesthood because they mistakenly viewed the requirement of celibacy as a means of avoiding struggles with their sexual identities. Others may have felt it provided them with "cover" -- a ready explanation as to why they were not married. One psychiatrist opined that some troubled priests felt "You could hide your sexual problem in the priesthood." One cleric echoed this view: "My fears about celibacy in the present world is that it can become a place for people with sexual disorders to hide."

The Review Board therefore believes that bishops must exercise exceptional care in the selection of candidates for admission to the seminaries, to ensure that individuals ill-suited for the demands of the priesthood are screened out before the commencement of a process at which they are likely to fail and before they are placed in a position where they could pose a risk of harm to minors.

A candidate for the priesthood must have proper training to understand the meaning of celibacy and guidance on how to live a celibate life. It must be presented as one with the entire Catholic sexual ethic. The Review Board believes this is a critical aspect of the formation process discussed at greater length above. The celibate life is especially difficult in our culture today, where the perception is, as one bishop put it, that "unless you're sexually active, you're not an adult."

According to *Pastores Dabo Vobis*, "Of the greatest importance for formation for chastity in celibacy are the bishop's concern and fraternal life among priests." (*Pastores Dabo Vobis* ¶ 50.) Thus, as part of seminary training, "celibacy should be presented clearly, without any ambiguities, and in a positive fashion." (*Id.*) Yet, as one priest, stated, "Very few bishops sit down with the priests and say, 'What's it like being celibate?' I don't mean, 'Are you having an affair right now?' But, 'What kind of a struggle has it been, or has it been easy?'" The Review Board believes that avoiding discussions of this topic contributed to an environment where a priest having difficulty with celibacy was more likely to find an unhealthy (and possibly criminal) outlet for his frustrations, thereby providing fuel for the current crisis, however unwittingly.

To be a successful celibate, one must understand the meaning and purpose of priestly celibacy. Priestly celibacy is not simply an unmarried state or even refraining from sexual relations – although it is obviously both of those things. Rather, as Pope Paul VI wrote, priestly celibacy is intended to enable the priest to further model Christ, to espouse himself to the Church, and to serve as a sacrifice for the entire People of God. (*Sacerdotalis Caelibatus* ¶¶ 17-34.) As one bishop explained, successful celibacy requires more than simply saying "No" to sex:

> I don't think celibacy is the problem unless you understand it as bachelorhood and as a kind of unhealthy bachelorhood. . . . Celibacy has got to be understood relationally. You cannot be a good celibate without some intimacy in your life. You cannot be a good celibate

85

unless you can relate equally well to women and men and have friendships among women and men. You cannot be a good celibate without
a prayer life, without a confessor and a spiritual director.

It appears that too many priests and too many bishops acted as if
celibacy was something that could be imposed as part of the formation process and
then taken for granted. Whether such an approach ever was possible, it is clear that
in the hyper-sexualized American society of the past few decades, living a celibate
life takes commitment and dedication on a daily basis both before and after ordination. As Pope John Paul II has noted, priests who have given a promise or a vow of
celibacy still must struggle with desires and yearnings just like all humans: "Since
the charism of celibacy, even when it is genuine and has proved itself, leaves one's
affections and instinctive impulses intact, candidates to the priesthood need an
affective maturity which is prudent, able to renounce anything that is a threat to it,
vigilant over both body and spirit, and capable of esteem and respect in interpersonal
relationships between men and women." (*Pastores Dabo Vobis* ¶ 44.)

As with so many aspects of the crisis, the interaction of celibacy
cannot be isolated from cultural changes in American society. Reflecting this, one
bishop said that living a celibate life always has been a "struggle" for priests, but that
it is an even greater struggle today because the "culture and the community" no
longer "sustain it." That is, whereas living a celibate life was once more generally
appreciated as heroic, today often it is seen as peculiar or even perverse. Another

bishop told the Board that the most healthy celibate is probably the one who struggles most with his human sexuality, and who every day has to say "yes to celibacy." According to this bishop and others, to maintain his vow of celibacy, a priest needs (i) a solid prayer life; (ii) friendship with peers, married and unmarried, clergy and laity; and (iii) job satisfaction.

The effect of the discipline of celibacy on the behavior of priests should be viewed in light of the reality that priests traditionally have not been subject to close oversight. For young priests who had just left the rigid pre-Vatican II seminary, where they were under constant scrutiny, becoming an assistant pastor at a parish was a liberation. These individuals suddenly were respected and trusted without question, and just as suddenly given responsibility for dealing with youth groups. This abrupt change, both in increased responsibility and decreased oversight, increased the risk of sexual misconduct by priests – particularly those who were not properly selected and trained. The lack of oversight is particularly troubling. According to one priest: "I see my bishop four times a year at public gatherings. I could have a concubine and three children and nobody would know it except the housekeeper in the rectory." The Board believes that each bishop should know his priests and he should consider, as another priest suggested, following a policy of meeting personally and privately with each of his priests at least once or twice a year.

Unlike religious order priests who take a vow of celibacy but live in community with other priests of the order, many diocesan priests live alone in isolated rectories with little sense of community or oversight and thus may lack some of the emotional benefits afforded by a sense of community. This isolation in some instances may have afforded some priests the freedom to commit acts of abuse without detection. Religious order priests often comment that they believe it is easier for them to live a celibate life because they live in a community that provides them support and intimacy. Diocesan living arrangements bear revisiting in light of the scandal of sexual abuse of minors by priests. Several witnesses recommended that dioceses consider establishing residential living centers for priests that would help to meet the twin purposes of fostering community and healthy intimate relationships and ensuring oversight of priests. Indeed, such a living situation for diocesan priests is highly recommended by the Code of Canon Law in Canon 280.

Although beyond the scope of this Report, there are a number of other issues relating to celibacy that could provide a breeding ground for other crises. For example, numerous witnesses told the Board that they believe there were more incidents of sexual relationships between a priest and a consenting adult woman or man than between a priest and a minor. Although it is typically not a crime to engage in sexual relations with a consenting adult, men and women involved in sexual affairs with priests are often vulnerable, and in any event such conduct by a priest is gravely immoral. Bishops and other church leaders cannot allow such conduct to occur without consequences. Statements to the effect that it is "nobody's business" if a priest engages in sexual conduct with an adult are fundamentally wrong. Whether a priest keeps his vows and lives in accordance with the moral precepts of the Church is the business of his bishop, his fellow priests, and his parishioners.

*      *      *

In sum, there can be no doubt that while it is a gift for some, celibacy is a terrible burden for others, resulting in loneliness, alcohol and drug abuse, and improper sexual conduct. That does not mean, of course, that celibacy should not remain a principle of priestly life. Living a celibate life can allow a priest to model Christ more fully and to commit himself completely to his people in a way that many believe would not be possible if the priest were married. And many priests firmly believe that, as one priest stated, the "genuine sacrifice" of celibacy "can be converted into a form of prayer that provides additional grace to others who may be struggling with various problems."

It would be presumptuous of the Review Board, and beyond its mandate, to opine on the relative merits of a celibate or non-celibate priesthood. But it is clear that bishops must remain watchful to ensure that priests embrace chaste celibacy as part of their priestly identity and not as a burden imposed upon them or as a means of escape or denial. In addition, because celibacy is widely misunderstood by the American public, the Church must take care to address issues relating to celibacy in an open and forthright manner.

The Board also notes that dioceses in the United States today vary widely in their treatment of priests who violate their vows of celibacy in situations that do not involve abuse of minors, and that the Church would be well advised to consider establishing guidelines for addressing such lapses that would bring greater clarity to the meaning of celibacy, both for priests and the public. Finally, the Board believes that greater examination by the Church of the role of, extent of compliance with, and consequences of celibacy would be beneficial given the ramifications of celibacy with respect to many aspects of Church life. It is a subject that demands further study.

## 5. Special Issues Relating to Spiritual Life.

While there are many ways to view the current crisis, as a crisis of priestly identity or a crisis of episcopal leadership, the Board believes that the overriding paradigm that characterizes the crisis is one of sinfulness. The actions of priests who sexually abused minors were grievously sinful. The inaction of those bishops who failed to protect their people from predators was also grievously sinful. Somehow, the "smoke of Satan" was allowed to enter the Church, and as a result the Church itself has been deeply wounded. Its ability to speak clearly and credibly on moral issues has been seriously impaired.

90

The only way to combat sinfulness is with holiness. This is not a public relations battle for the approval of the press or the loyalty of the laity. It is, fundamentally, the age-old issue of good and evil. The Church must be holy; her ministers must be holy; her people must be holy. The foundation of holiness is a strong spiritual life, a life of prayer and simplicity. Priests who were truly holy would not have abused young people; nor would they have allowed others to do so.

In this regard, individuals who have spoken with priest perpetrators note that sexual misconduct typically followed a failure to maintain a daily prayer life. A priest is not a social worker or a youth counselor. A priest brings the word of God to the People of God, and this is not possible without a strong spiritual life.

In sum, as Pope John Paul II emphasized in his address to the U.S. bishops in 1993 on the sexual abuse of minors by clergy, "this whole sad question must be placed in a context which is not exclusively human." Because of this, of the many necessary responses to the scandal, "the first and most important is prayer: ardent, humble, confident prayer."

B.     **The Response of U.S. Church Officials to Sexual Abuse of Minors By Priests.**

Although the fact that approximately four percent of clergy have sexually abused minors outrages and saddens the laity, the overwhelming majority of the clergy have led honorable lives of dedication to the Church and her people. More distressing to the laity is the inadequate response by bishops and other Church

91

leaders to this problem over the last twenty-five years. Too many bishops in the United States failed to respond to this problem forthrightly and firmly. Their responses were characterized by moral laxity, excessive leniency, insensitivity, secrecy, and neglect. Aspects of the failure to respond properly to sexual abuse of minors by priests included: (i) inadequately dealing with victims of clergy sexual abuse, both pastorally and legally; (ii) allowing offending priests to remain in positions of risk; (iii) transferring offending priests to new parishes or other dioceses without informing others of their histories; (iv) failing to report instances of criminal conduct by priests to secular law enforcement authorities, whether such a report was required by law or not; and (v) declining to take steps to laicize priests who clearly had violated canon law.

Most fundamentally, some bishops in the United States did not appreciate the gravity of the problem of sexual abuse of minors by clergy. Until recently, these bishops all too often treated victims of clerical sexual abuse as adversaries and threats to the well-being of the Church, not as injured parishioners in need of healing. Far too frequently, they treated predator priests as misdirected individuals in need of psychological treatment or a simple change in environment, rather than as criminal offenders to be removed from ministry and reported to civil authorities for possible prosecution and appropriate punishment. These approaches did not solve any problems but rather served to exacerbate them.

92

Certain bishops and other Church leaders in the United States were altogether too easy on their fellow clergy and too willing to take the easy way out themselves. All of the presumptions weighed in favor of the accused priest at the expense of the victim. This tilt is attributable in part to "clericalism" – an attitude that priests and bishops are apart from and superior to the laity – and in part to idiosyncracies in canon law. In addition, the failure of some bishops to exercise proper governance, choosing instead to minimize or rationalize or forgive or just ignore misconduct, or else to pass along problems to other unsuspecting dioceses, has led to governmental intervention that could threaten the independence of the Church in the United States. The civil authorities, when dealing with the Church, must be sensitive to this concern and should take pains to ensure that they do not unnecessarily intrude upon internal workings of the Church, which are protected by the First Amendment's guarantee of free exercise of religion. For its part, Church leaders must understand that a failure properly to police themselves simply invites this type of governmental intrusion.

### 1. Understanding the Nature and Scope of the Abuse and the Harm it Caused.

Church leaders failed to appreciate the harm suffered by victims of sexual abuse by priests, the seriousness of the underlying misconduct, and the frequency of the abuse. In the 1950s and early 1960s, many Church leaders viewed sexual abuse as a moral lapse only and did not understand the psychological causes

93

and consequences of such conduct. More recently, some Church leaders viewed sexual abuse as a psychological problem only and placed undue reliance on therapy as a solution. The failure of Church leaders to recognize sexual abuse of minors as a crime, and not just the manifestation of a moral failing and psychological disorder, and to deal with it accordingly, has contributed enormously to the current crisis.

Many bishops and other Church leaders either did not feel or did not express the sense of outrage experienced so overwhelmingly by the broader community at the heinous acts committed by priests under their authority.[39] Their failure to exercise their authority in a manner that properly redressed past abuse and precluded further abuse has badly compromised the ability of the Church to play a leadership role with respect to important contemporary moral issues.

Many Church leaders appeared to have avoided dealing with problems of sexual abuse, perhaps because of a discomfort about addressing sexual issues and a reluctance to exercise their authority over priests, often leaving to others with less authority the management of critical issues they should have addressed themselves.

---

[39] The lack of expressions of outrage by bishops – both at the time they first learned of the abhorrent acts of some priests and in dealing with the crisis publicly – is troubling. The Board has seen no letters condemning the men who have engaged in such conduct. To the contrary, Cardinal Law's letter in 1996 placing Geoghan on "sick leave" concludes by expressing the Cardinal's "warmest personal regards," and Cardinal Law's letter later that year accepting Geoghan's request for retirement states, "Yours has been an effective life of ministry, sadly impaired by illness."

In addition, some bishops delegated this responsibility. For example, it is clear from the Review Board's examination of the Boston Archdiocese that Cardinal Law paid insufficient personal attention to the problem of sexual abuse of minors by priests under his authority and that the clerics to whom he delegated responsibility for this issue often failed in their handling of it. Nor did Cardinal Law properly supervise those to whom he delegated authority, essentially abdicating responsibility for a matter of paramount importance to the integrity of the Church. As one bishop said of Cardinal Law, "I think he wasn't even paying attention."

Many in the Church failed to realize or appreciate that sexual conduct by an adult with an older minor is a criminal act. As a result of this failure to appreciate the legal (as well as moral) dimension of this conduct, clergy abuse of minors was very rarely reported to the civil authorities. One priest stated, "I just don't think it ever occurred to them that there was a law out there; that the ethos of the society was that . . . you go to prison for this." To the extent that bishops and provincials really did not comprehend that sexual conduct between an adult and an adolescent was a crime, the fault must lay somewhat with their legal counsel.

The Review Board recognizes that bishops have numerous obligations. But surely none of these should be allowed to take precedence over protecting children and young people whose religious instruction is entrusted to their care, or to preclude responding to problems that threaten the well-being of the presbyterate itself. It may be true that some bishops were not aware of numerous allegations against priests under their supervision, but that is no defense – instead, it is part and parcel of the problem. Ignorance is no excuse here. As one victim of clergy sexual abuse said to the Board, bishops must be told, "Sir, it's your job to know what's going on. It's your job to know what happened."

Even a bishop with responsibilities for the administration of hundreds of parishes and big-picture issues such as social and economic justice or respect for life cannot allow those responsibilities to eclipse his fundamental duty to ensure that each of the people of his diocese is in the care of a good pastor. "The best thing you ever do as a bishop is to give a parish a good priest," one bishop told us. Unfortunately, as we have seen, not all bishops appear to have shared or acted on that view.

### 2.    Responding to Victims.

The first role of a bishop or any other Church leader must be to act as a pastor to the Catholic faithful. When faced with allegations by parishioners of abuse by clerics, however, far too many Church leaders did not deal with victims in a pastoral fashion. As one survivor of clergy sexual abuse told the Board, what victims typically want is to be "treated with respect and dignity." In too many cases, however, victims were marginalized and, in effect, re-victimized.

As noted above, far too few bishops grasped the severity of the harm experienced by victims of clergy sexual abuse, particularly minors. Several victims have committed suicide. Others have struggled for decades with psychological complications of the abuse, including depression, drug dependency, and sexual dysfunction. These effects often do not manifest themselves for years. One victim told us that the "shame and the guilt" borne of clerical sexual abuse is "so strong that people keep it silent for years, well into adulthood."[40] Victims who came forward and told their story showed tremendous courage, as was clear to the Board from meeting with many of them.

The Review Board believes the failure to understand the harm is attributable, in large measure, to the fact that bishops and other Church leaders rarely spoke personally with victims of sexual abuse, in part, as discussed more fully below, in misplaced reliance upon myopic legal advice. Time and again, bishops informed the Board that they did not fully comprehend the horror of sexual abuse and the damage it wrought until they had met with a number of victims. As one said, "Anyone should have seen the horror of it. But unless you listen to victims, survivors, you don't really have that sense of the horror." Another bishop said that there was "a disconnect whereby for some reason at a pastoral level bishops and priests did not grasp how horrified the average parent would be over the thought that his or her child would be sexually abused by a member of the clergy."

---

[40]     For this reason, it may be too soon to know whether the significant decrease in the number of reported incidents of sexual abuse of minors over the last twenty years represents as great a decrease in the actual number of incidents.

Sexual abuse inherently is traumatic; and when committed by a priest, it is especially traumatic. Because a priest is quite literally a "father figure," abuse by a priest is likely to cause more harm to a child than abuse by any other individual outside of the family. Moreover, a unique consequence of abuse by a member of the clergy is the damage to the victim's faith. Indeed, some priests committed these crimes in connection with the sacrament of confession or in relation to other Church liturgies, aggravating the spiritual damage. Abusing priests also have, by their conduct, made many victims feel that it is difficult, if not impossible, to remain in communion with the Church or indeed to hold any religious belief.[41]

Many Church leaders refused to meet with victim support groups because they disagreed with the agendas of some of these groups. Although some members of victim support groups are not always fair to the bishops and are unwilling to give credit when it is due, disregarding these groups is short-sighted and contributes to the perception of a closed and secretive Church. Distaste for the messenger too often blinded Church leadership to the significance of the message. It should come as no surprise that many victims and their friends and families feel alienated from the institutional Church and turn to support groups that appear hostile

---

[41]     As Bishop D'Arcy noted in one of his letters from the early 1980s to archdiocesan authorities in Boston raising concerns about priests who had sexually abused young boys, "Young people are open to priests and when assaulted in this way, their souls are often irreparably damaged."

to it. The Review Board believes that the proper response of the Church in these circumstances is to strive for rapprochement and reconciliation, and not to interpose rejection or condemnation.

The failure to meet with victims often resulted in bishops making decisions based on a one-sided version of events. As one bishop said to the Board: "Bishops are human. Sometimes they get diffident about walking into situations where they don't know what's going to be waiting for them there, and so they back off and say, 'Well, maybe I won't go there; but here, I know this priest and I'll talk to him.'" It should have been obvious that talking only to priests about allegations against priests was unlikely to provide an adequate basis for determining the validity of allegations and responding to a problem of enormous magnitude.

The Review Board believes that bishops should seek to participate in face-to-face meetings with victims and their families whenever possible. As one bishop told us, these meetings help both the victims and the bishops by providing solace to the former and catharsis for the latter. And as another bishop observed: "I think if we can't talk to people and listen to people, then we're in the wrong business." Yet one bishop who had served as a diocesan official told us that he had been reprimanded by a diocesan attorney for speaking to victims and saying that he was sorry for what the victim had suffered.

The importance of a holistic approach should not be underestimated. Parents of victims can feel angry at the Church while also feeling guilty that they did not prevent their child from being harmed. Often, too, they feel ashamed that their child did not tell them what happened or that they responded poorly when told by their child. The full range of these emotions must be addressed, however painfully, if bishops truly are to fulfill their pastoral responsibilities.

In sum, failure to meet with victims and their families prevented bishops from comprehending the nature and the scope of the problem. More importantly, those Church leaders who did not meet with victims and their families, and did not endeavor to bring healing to them, failed in their pastoral duties. This failure of the Catholic clergy to attend to the pain of its parishioners is all the more egregious inasmuch as the underlying injury was inflicted by a member of the clergy itself.

### 3. Presumptions in Favor of Accused Priests.

A significant cause of the inadequate response of Church leaders to allegations of sexual abuse was the fact that in assessing allegations against accused priests, presumptions rooted in both theology and Church culture heavily favored the accused priest. Surveying the landscape in certain dioceses, one bishop noted, "There is a larger pattern of protection of priests first, rather than protecting the children first."

### a. The Presumed Right to Ministry.

Under Church doctrine, when a man is ordained as a priest he is permanently marked with the sign of Christ and ontologically changed. That is, unless the ordination was somehow invalid, a priest is always a priest, even if laicized. This concept gave rise to an unfounded perception that a priest had a "right" to his ministry and caused unwillingness or reluctance on the part of bishops to take steps to remove a priest from ministry. This reluctance may have been reinforced by a view that regardless of other conduct, through the power of his ordination, a priest still was able to perform his essential function – that is, to offer mass and administer the sacraments.

But even if a priest had not been formally laicized, there were no bars, theological or otherwise, to excluding him from public ministry. To a degree, orders may have found it easier than dioceses did to deal with problem priests in this regard. A diocesan priest typically is a parish priest, and the dioceses do not have a significant number of non-ministry positions to which priests can be assigned. By contrast, the typical religious house has a variety of positions that involve no ministry or contact with children.

### b. The Process of Laicization Under the Code of Canon Law.

Canon law long has provided that a priest can be laicized for engaging in sexual abuse of a minor. Nevertheless, bishops and religious ordinaries very rarely

101

responded to evidence of a violation of canon law by resorting to a canonical charge, in part because canon law procedures made it very difficult to take action against a priest. As one bishop told the Board, "I'm not a canon lawyer, but I happen to think that the Code of Canon Law we've got is flawed. . . . I just think it's so much weighted toward the rights of the individual that the common good of the Church is not adequately protected." Indeed, canon law experts have informed the Board that, prior to the adoption of the Essential Norms, there were exceptionally few cases in which priests who had engaged in sexual abuse of minors were dismissed from the clerical state as a result of the diocesan panel process stipulated in canon law.

Canon law has proven to be an inadequate method of dealing with cases of sexual abuse of minors for many reasons. First, the canonical tribunals in dioceses simply did not have the expertise to handle involuntary laicization cases. These tribunals dealt almost exclusively with annulment cases. The canonists in the tribunals had little training in the canons and procedures relating to punishment of clerics, including Canon 1395. The Board interviewed several individuals with degrees in canon law, and the remarks of one regarding laicization provisions captured the views of many: "This was seen as something very extreme and so you probably wouldn't be using it very much. At least that was the impression that I got when we were studying it." In hindsight, the Church would have been better served if a national canonical tribunal or regional tribunals had been established to hear and decide cases involving abuse by priests. Within the past year, such regional tribunals have been proposed to hear laicization cases in the wake of the implementation of the Essential Norms.

The canon law process for dealing with sexual abuse cases was impeded further by the concept of "imputability," which provided that the penalty of laicization could not be handed down if the priest or his advocate were able to show that the priest was not completely responsible for his actions because of an illness or some other psychological condition. Thus, the worst predators, who actually had been diagnosed as pedophiles or as suffering from some other "illness," paradoxically were the most difficult to laicize under canon law. Evidence that the priest was under the influence of alcohol also could serve as a mitigating factor.

In addition, process often took precedence over substance. Under canon law, some convictions could be reversed by tribunals in Rome years after the fact because of a failure to follow all technical procedural requirements, injecting the potential for inordinate delays into cases that did go forward. One bishop told us that his fellow bishops avoided recourse to canon law because they "weren't sure where Rome would come down," adding that "it was extremely hard to press your case in Rome and be sure that you would be heard." Another told the Board, "We were all very hesitant to do a canonical trial because if there's any procedural flaw in it you can easily be overturned on appeal to Rome."

103

Reportedly, the Vatican courts tended to err on the side of protecting a priest because of a concern that bishops could seek to use canon law to rid themselves of priests whom they did not like or with whom they disagreed on some point or another. The focus of the law and of the canonists interpreting and applying the law historically was on protecting the rights of the accused. Although the Review Board believes it is important to protect the rights of accused priests, it also believes that greater consideration must be given to the protection of the faithful.

###     c.        Clericalism.

Clerical culture and a misplaced sense of loyalty made some priests look the other way in the face of evidence of sexual abuse of minors, and contributed to the unwillingness of members of the clergy to condemn the conduct of a brother priest. Some witnesses likened the clerical culture to a feudal or a military culture and said that priests and bishops who "rocked the boat" were less likely to advance. Likewise, we were told, some bishops did not want to be associated with any problem for fear of criticism because problems arose on their watch. As a result, problems were left to fester.

Clericalism also contributed to a culture of secrecy. In many instances, Church leaders valued confidentiality and a priest's right to privacy above the prevention of further harm to victims and the vindication of their rights. Both confidentiality and privacy are valuable, and obviously it is important to take steps to ensure, to the extent possible, the privacy and rights of the accused. But these values should not be allowed to trump the duty to keep children safe from harm or to investigate claims of sexual abuse against clerics and respond appropriately.

Until recently, few dioceses relied on qualified independent fact-finders to assist in assessing the validity of allegations. Indeed, in some cases, the cleric making the decision about the future of a priest had known the priest for many years. For example, in Boston, the priest assigned responsibility for interviewing other priests accused of abuse and determining their credibility was a friend or seminary classmate of some of the accused priests. Moreover, the investigating official did not hear directly from the victim accusers. Rather, a woman religious spoke to victims and a priest spoke to accused priests. Although the nun found the victims almost uniformly to be credible, she played no role in deciding whether to return a priest to ministry; whereas those who participated in that decision had contact only with the accused, and were predisposed to believe self-serving assertions that no wrongdoing had occurred.

Clericalism also can be blamed for the fact that, to a great degree, bishops and other Church leaders engaged in massive denial. Church leaders often were reluctant to acknowledge that a priest, a man ordained to be "another Christ," could have engaged in the horrific acts of which he was accused. Thus, some diocesan leaders were too willing to accept exculpatory explanations by priests even when it appeared that the accuser was credible. With the benefit of hindsight, it appears that many of the clerics charged with investigating accused priests were either incredibly naive or willing to look the other way. Indeed, Church officials seemed to want to keep information from themselves. One priest who tried to bring his concerns about clergy sexual abuse of minors to his bishop in a letter was chastised by the vicar general for doing so. "It was," the priest asserts, "total denial."

Finally, the haughty attitude of some bishops, which has exacerbated the crisis, is a byproduct of clericalism. Just as priests are often placed on a pedestal far above the laity that they serve, certain bishops appear far removed from their priests. As several exemplary bishops have displayed in responding to the crisis, a bishop must lead with humility, not hubris, and never forget that he is first and foremost a pastor to his people.

### d.      Forgiveness Without Condemnation.

Even where the evidence of misconduct was incontrovertible, many bishops felt compelled to forgive the offending priest so long as that priest appeared contrite. Clearly, where brother priests were concerned, bishops often felt more comfortable forgiving than condemning, even where condemnation was demanded by the nature of the offense. This eagerness to forgive (and forget) failed to take into account the harm the offending priest had caused and the potential for repeated violations. Jesus did not fail to condemn when condemnation was called for.

106

Indeed, speaking of children, he said that "anyone who is the downfall of one of these little ones who have faith in me would be better drowned in the depths of the sea with a great millstone around his neck." (Matthew 18:6.) The laity expect bishops likewise to condemn when necessary, both in public statements and in private conversations with their priests.

Forgiveness is not incompatible with consequences as the concept of penance clearly shows. But too many bishops and other Church leaders simply forgave the errant priest, in effect immunizing, rather than punishing, conduct that violated both canon and civil law. And too many were too willing to accept without question the word of predator priests who voiced repentance and then, immune from any consequences for past misconduct, went on to repeat their criminal sins.[42]

### 4. Secrecy and the Avoidance of Scandal.

Faced with serious and potentially inflammatory abuses, Church leaders placed too great an emphasis on the avoidance of scandal in order to protect the reputation of the Church, which ultimately bred far greater scandal and reputational injury. One bishop opined that because the Church in the United States historically is a minority, immigrant institution, it has been particularly desirous of

---

[42]  Some bishops and priests believe that the scandal is cause to re-examine confessional practices. The seal of confession must never be violated, but a priest hearing a confession that involves the commission of a crime has the authority to withhold absolution subject to certain conditions, such as turning oneself into the authorities or seeking help for a problem.

seeking to solve its own problems without exposing them to a hostile culture. Several others echoed this thought. This desire to keep problems "within the family" also may have stemmed from a shortsighted concern that the faith of the laity would be shaken by their exposure. At heart, this was a failure of Church leadership, which lacked the vision to recognize that, unless nipped in the bud, the problems would only grow until they no longer could be contained, and that then the problems would have an even greater propensity to undermine the faith of the laity.

The impulse to avoid scandal at all costs manifested itself in several ways. First, Church leaders kept information from parishioners and other dioceses that should have been provided to them. Some also pressured victims not to inform the authorities or the public of abuse. For example, some dioceses did not inform parishioners when allegations about a priest who had served at that parish arose, although such a practice might have given additional victims the courage to come forward and would have helped the diocese determine the validity of complaints. Bishops and other Church leaders often did not tell their brethren the full story when a priest took up residence in a new diocese, and the bishop in the receiving diocese often did not ask all of the questions about the incoming priest that he should have asked. This lack of candor – with parishioners, with civil authorities, with fellow bishops – avoided scandal in the short term while sowing seeds for greater upheaval in the long term.

The Review Board is concerned that, even today, some bishops and priests fail to address the issue of clerical sexual abuse in a sufficiently open manner. Bishops and priests have a duty to bring others to the gospel. Given the highly public profile of the current crisis, that evangelization must include addressing the scandal of clergy sexual abuse of minors. The Church must inform current parishioners and potential converts of the steps that the Church has taken and is taking to deal with both the causes of clergy sexual abuse of minors and its consequences. Yet, with some notable exceptions, priests and bishops still shy away from the subject and revert to defensive postures.[43] Such a stance will do little to renew the trust of the laity or encourage others to learn more about the Catholic faith.

Four implications of the impulse to avoid scandal are particularly troubling to the Review Board in the context of the current crisis. First, time and again Church leaders failed to report incidents of possible criminal activity to the civil authorities.[44] In fairness, at the time, Church leaders typically were not required

---

[43] One such exception is a diocese in which the bishop asked all of his pastors to show a video on the sexual abuse crisis during mass. In addition, parishioners received copies of a special bulletin devoted to this issue. Such actions cannot be viewed simply as damage control; rather, such outreach to parishioners on this issue is an important part of the Church's mission to strengthen and spread the faith.

[44] In discussing the reluctance of some bishops to report the conduct of priests to the authorities one bishop noted the "father-son" relationship between a bishop and the priests he ordains. Surely, however, even a father must take

(continued...)

to report allegations of sexual abuse of minors to civil authorities. In addition, civil authorities often showed little interest in receiving information about cases that were beyond the statute of limitations. But it is clear in hindsight that the Church could have prevented numerous acts of sexual abuse had its leaders reported all allegations of sexual abuse by priests to the civil authorities. Where the evidence warranted, offenders could have been prosecuted and punished before they were able to perpetuate their misconduct; and by their example, other priests could have been deterred from engaging in similar misconduct. Article 4 of the Charter requires dioceses to report allegations of sexual abuse of a minor, even when not required by law to report, and to "cooperate with public authorities about reporting in cases when the person is no longer a minor." The Board believes that dioceses should report all such cases to civil authorities, regardless of whether the victim is still a minor or not.

Second, in some instances Church leaders discouraged victims or their parents from reporting the abuse to authorities. Again Article 4 now requires dioceses to "advise victims of their right to make a report to public authorities" and to support this right. Alternatively, victims or their families did not go to law enforcement because they trusted the Church to take care of the problem. That trust

---

[44]    (...continued)
steps to prevent his son from harming others if put in a position to do so.

repeatedly was breached, in itself a serious failing; and the public disclosure of that breach has magnified the loss of faith on the part of some of the laity.

Third, certain witnesses stated that in some instances bishops may not have punished priests who engaged in sexual abuse because the bishops were themselves compromised. That is, priests either explicitly or implicitly threatened to reveal compromising information about a bishop if the bishop took steps against the priest. It should go without saying that any priest who believes that there is a basis upon which he could be subject to blackmail should not allow himself to be elevated to bishop or placed in any other position of authority.

Finally, in part out of an overemphasis on secrecy, dioceses and religious orders did not utilize adequate methods to track allegations against priests. Because records relating to an individual priest often would be kept in three or four separate files, Church leaders investigating allegations of sexual abuse by an individual priest did not always have all of the information they needed in order to assess the credibility of the allegations. Important documents often were maintained in "secret archives" pursuant to canon law, and Church officials without access to these files often were unaware of critical past allegations against a priest when addressing other allegations. Reflecting this, Cardinal Law at one point put the blame for the transfer of predator priests in part on an inadequate filing system.

The Review Board believes that dioceses and religious orders must maintain more open and accurate personnel records regarding priests, which should be audited and reviewed by diocesan lay boards or outside auditors. Nevertheless, the existence of a bad filing system only partially explains, and in no way excuses, the failing of various dioceses to respond properly to evidence of sexual abuse by members of their clergy. Had bishops placed the issue of sexual abuse of minors by the clergy at the top of their agenda, we have no doubt that the filing system on priest perpetrators would have been improved.

### 5. Dependence on the Therapeutic Model.

Bishops were too willing to turn over the problem of sexual abuse of minors to psychiatrists and psychologists. Moreover, even after the inherent limitations of treatment became well recognized, Church leaders continued to accept favorable reports as a basis, without any other considerations, to return perpetrators of abuse to positions of ministry.

To a certain degree, the response of many bishops demonstrates, as one witness stated, "the triumph of the bureaucratic and therapeutic over the theological." As discussed in greater detail below, even where the priest was removed from ministry on a temporary basis, some bishops were too ready to seize upon optimistic statements by therapists in deciding whether to return a priest to ministry. Some Church leaders withheld important and damaging information from treatment centers. Others solicited second opinions where the prognosis offered by the first professional was not to their liking, or relied on treatment centers that were more likely to provide a clean bill of health. This excessive dependence upon therapy, and worse, skewing of its outcome, compromised the ability of Church leaders to evaluate properly the prospective role of priests who had engaged in the sexual abuse of minors.

A psychiatric evaluation has limits, and the result of such an evaluation is only one of the factors that a bishop should consider in determining a priest's future. In a 1990 letter to a diocesan official, one psychiatrist underscored that the responsibility for determining whether to allow a priest to return to ministry, or to continue in any other capacity within the Church, belongs with the bishop and not the treatment center:

> We [psychiatrists] are certainly in a weak position when we try to make predictions about future behavior. . . . Because of the inherent weakness in the psychiatric assessment in determining whether or not an event has occurred, or may occur in the future, it is important that a separate administrative procedure, or internal due process procedure be established within an organization to deal with concerns about aberrant behavior. . . . A psychiatric evaluation can be helpful in providing information about whether or not a mental illness exists, but such an evaluation cannot be the determining factor in deciding what administrative action should be taken.

Reiterating this point, one bishop told the Board, "I don't think any bishop has the right to blame [treatment centers] for anything because the ultimate decision is the bishop's, not theirs."

113

Nonetheless, the Review Board is aware that other psychiatrists and psychologists have been willing to state, to bishops or other diocesan authorities, that priests who had sexually abused minors, and then had undergone treatment, did not pose a threat if returned to ministry. For example, one treatment center in 1989 diagnosed Father Geoghan as having "atypical pedophilia" and stated that he was "psychologically fit" to continue working with children. One assessment letter for another priest from another center indicated that the priest "is ready for re-assignment in the archdiocese" and that the priest would "do well in 'a solo project', provided that the Doctor's recommendations could be followed; *i.e.*, not too lonely and isolated a place, and with the provision that he keep in touch with the Doctor from time to time." It is not surprising that such vague recommendations resulted in simply returning priests to ministry with little follow-up or oversight.

An early 1990s report to a bishop from one therapist is almost effusive in praise of the patient, a priest who had engaged in sexual abuse of minors. After noting the "impressive improvement" shown by the priest in therapy, the letter states that the priest "has been a deeply frightened man, quick to cover his own spontaneity, and has suffered a significant degree of sexual confusion which has marred his ability to adjust as an adult to his social and intimate relationships." The letter goes on to note that it is "deeply gratifying to me as his therapist to witness his emergence from deep-seated shame and guilt," anticipates "an excellent outcome from his stay here," and thanks the bishop for "sending this courageous, talented man to us." The letter concludes, "It has been a privilege to know him."

Letters such as these and others, many of which have been made public as a result of litigation and government investigations, show that the staffs of treatment centers must shoulder some of the blame for decisions to allow priests who had abused minors to return to positions where they were able to repeat their offenses. A man who has sexually abused minors ought to be filled with "deep-seated shame and guilt," and bishops ought not to have countenanced such coddling of criminals. Indeed, a few treating physicians actually told bishops that returning a priest-perpetrator to ministry was a necessary part of that priest's recovery. One psychiatrist told the Board that it was not until the 1980s that treatment professionals realized that "part of successful treatment is to not put these folks out into situations where they would be tempted and where innocent children can be harmed." The Review Board believes, however, that Church leaders should have recognized sooner the inherent limitations of treatment, as well as the inflated sense of accomplishment displayed by some treatment centers.

Indeed, the Review Board found that treatment centers upon which Church leaders elected to rely – almost all of which were Church affiliated – had a vested interest in an ability to "cure" pedophiles and other individuals who had engaged in sexual abuse so that the centers would continue to receive referrals.

115

Because the objective of the referral to the treatment center, whether express or implied, was the return of the patient to the priesthood, there was little if any incentive to help a priest realize he could not return to the priesthood or to prepare him for life outside the priesthood. The lack of alternative treatment goals increased the propensity of some treatment centers to become advocates for the patient priests, as seen in the letters excerpted above. Although some treatment centers assert that the recidivism rate for those offenders who went through treatment was low, no reliable objective data is available on the rate of recidivism of priests who received treatment at particular centers. According to the diocesan officials familiar with the treatment centers, some had markedly worse records than others.[45]

Moreover, psychologists and psychiatrists told the Board that, since the mid to late 1980s, it generally has been understood that men who have engaged in frequent sexual abuse of minors can be treated but not cured. But many Church leaders continued to rely on reports of successful treatment as a license to return

---

[45]    Dioceses tended to rely on treatment centers affiliated with the Church that treated only priests. It appears that some of these centers may have been less rigorous than non-affiliated treatment centers, either in their treatment or in their willingness to opine about the priest's suitability for continued ministry. In addition, it appears that many of the individuals previously managing certain treatment centers had notions of sexuality that at best could be termed inconsistent with Catholic teaching. In light of all this, it is now clear that no bishop or provincial should have sent a priest to any treatment center without having first assured himself, through background checks and other methods of verification, that the treatment being offered was effective.

priests to ministry. Won over by the promise of therapeutic cures, some bishops failed to recognize the typically compulsive and habitual nature of sexual abuse. This was understandable in the 1960s and 1970s, when even psychologists lacked a genuine understanding of the nature of sexual disorders. However, some bishops continued to return abusive priests to ministry after the compulsive nature of their afflictions became generally accepted within the medical profession. Many of the worst abusers were described as "manipulators" and "con artists," and it appears that they were able to con doctors and bishops as well as victims. In deciding their fate, however, bishops should have considered deeds, not words.

It also should be noted that, even when treatment centers indicated that an individual priest may no longer have presented a significant threat, the centers often based that assessment on an assumption that the priest would receive extensive post-treatment care in the form of counseling and monitoring. In reality, however, priests typically did not receive such follow-up care after returning to ministry from a stay in a treatment center. Through painful experience, dioceses learned that "supervised ministry" did not work because complete supervision was impossible.

In sum, by viewing sexual abuse with minors primarily as an issue of "psychosexual identity" and not primarily as a crime and a grave sin, bishops failed to fulfill their responsibilities to members of the public and members of the Church. Although psychiatry may play a role in diagnosis of sexual disorders and in treatment, some Church leaders appeared, as one bishop put it, to have replaced theology with psychiatry and to have shown, as another bishop stated, "a much greater willingness to accept the authority [of psychologists and psychiatrists] than their science or art justified."

The inherent limitations of treatment centers were aggravated by the fact that they were not always provided by the dioceses with all of the information about a priest that would be needed to diagnose and treat him properly. Sometimes, this was due to inadvertence on the part of referring dioceses, which often did not retain allegations about a priest in an organized fashion. However, it appears that on other occasions dioceses intentionally withheld information from treatment centers.

For example, the Archdiocese of Boston sent Father Geoghan to one particular treatment center for an evaluation in 1996. Although Geoghan already had been evaluated by at least two other treatment centers, and although several allegations relating to him were by that time in the files of the Archdiocese, the receiving center was not provided with Geoghan's full history. Through sheer coincidence, the Board was told, a psychologist from a different institution who had treated Geoghan previously was asked by the new center to evaluate him. Only then did the treating professionals hear about additional allegations relating to Geoghan. Of course, the fact that Geoghan was repeatedly referred to several different treatment centers is testament to the limitations of treatment as well as the Church's over-dependence on treatment as a way of dealing with predator priests.[46]

As noted above, in some instances, when confronted with unfavorable treatment reports, Church leaders sought second opinions in an apparent effort to be able to return a priest to ministry. Father Geoghan was returned to ministry at one point based merely on a letter written by his family physician, who hardly was qualified to assess whether he was afflicted with a threatening sexual disorder. Many problem priests were sent to multiple treatment centers. One priest with experience in dealing with priests who had sexually abused minors told the Review Board that some bishops "were actually looking for some kind of window from the psychologists that would allow them to reassign the priests in good conscience." The Review Board believes that this kind of opinion-shopping to enable a priest to return to ministry was an abdication of responsibility on the part of the bishops who engaged in it.

### 6. Reliance on Attorneys.

Many Church leaders tended to respond to allegations of sexual abuse of minors by clergy as a legal problem rather than as a pastoral problem. As a result,

---

[46]    In addition, the January 2003 report issued by the grand jury in Suffolk County, New York, stated that a Rockville Centre diocesan official acknowledged to the grand jury that treatment centers often were not provided with the complete file of a priest referred by the diocese to that treatment center for evaluation and treatment.

they relied too heavily on the advice of attorneys whose tactics often were inappropriate for the Church, and which tended to compound the effects of the abuse that already had been inflicted. These tactics included raising inappropriate defenses that could be construed as blaming the victim, such as assumption of risk or contributory negligence; disclaiming responsibility for their priests by claiming that they were "independent contractors"; and, in general, adopting an overly adversarial approach. Even when cases were being settled, certain lawyers recommended, and certain bishops insisted, that the victims sign confidentiality agreements, which stifled their ability to discuss their experience openly and thwarted awareness by the laity of the problem.

As a general matter, as one bishop observed, "the Church has not always been served well in a legal way." Indeed, it appears that many dioceses and orders made disastrous pastoral decisions relying on attorneys who failed to adapt their tactics to account for the unique role and responsibilities of the Church. In many instances, the selection of a diocesan attorney was based less on the ability of the lawyer and more on friendship and a misguided perception of the lawyer's loyalty to the Church.

In addition, neither dioceses nor U.S. Church leaders as a whole appeared to have developed a consistent, coordinated approach to dealing with the growing crisis and its litigation consequences. In this respect, the Conference could have served as a clearinghouse and strategic resource for the dioceses; but many dioceses did not seek guidance from the Conference. In some cases, dioceses settled cases for large sums without informing the Conference's General Counsel of the matter. As a result of this fractured approach, the problem was able to metastasize.

Many diocesan attorneys counseled Church leaders not to meet with, or apologize to, victims even when the allegations had been substantiated on grounds that apologies could be used against the Church in court. The Review Board believes that offering solace to those who have been harmed by a minister of the Church should have taken precedence over a potential incremental increase in the risk of liability. Moreover, the judgment that the risk would be increased itself was questionable. The views of one bishop on the reliance on attorneys in this regard are instructive:

> We made terrible mistakes. Because the attorneys said over and over "Don't talk to the victims, don't go near them," and here they were victims. I heard victims say "We would not have taken it to [plaintiffs' attorneys] had someone just come to us and said, "I'm sorry." But we listened to the attorneys.

In addition, while statutes of limitation serve a vital role in a system of ordered justice, it must be stressed that, as one victim told us, although the expiration of the statute of limitation "can be a vindication in terms of legal responsibility or even financial responsibility . . . morally as we stand as Christians and as a Church, it's no vindication."

121

Furthermore, many dioceses and orders refused to settle claims without a confidentiality clause that bound the victim from speaking about the abuse. Although such clauses are common in litigation settlements and victims or their attorneys often requested such clauses, the insistence by certain dioceses and orders on confidentiality agreements when settling claims of abuse brought by victims raises several concerns. First, confidentiality agreements made it less likely that other victims would come forward and provide the Church with additional information about a problem priest. Second, these agreements often hindered victims from healing by causing them to consider incidents of abuse shameful secrets. Third, the agreements deterred any restoration of faith in the Church by the victims and their families by reinforcing the perception that the Church was unwilling to take ownership of its problems. Fourth, the agreements contributed to an overall atmosphere of secrecy within the Church that prevented Church leaders from realizing the scope of the problem of clerical sexual abuse of minors. And finally, when it became known, predictably, that some dioceses had insisted on confidentiality as a condition of settlement in order to hide the existence and extent of sexual abuse of minors of priests, the public reaction to the crisis, again predictably, became substantially more negative.

In short, the Church cannot and should not hide behind its lawyers or the law blindly and in all circumstances. The words of one victim to the Board are plain and to the point: "Folks, this is the Catholic Church. People expect a higher moral standard."

### 7.    Considerations Relating to the Religious Orders.

Approximately one-third of the estimated 45,000 priests in the United States today are not diocesan priests under the direct authority of bishops but are instead members of religious orders and societies, such as the Jesuits, Dominicans, Franciscans, and others. Like certain dioceses, certain orders were plagued with a large number of priest offenders, and the leaders of the orders, known as major superiors or provincial superiors, often responded inadequately and inappropriately to the sexual abuse of minors by priests within their orders.

The Essential Norms apply equally to religious order priests and the leaders of religious orders, *mutatis mutandis*. However, the orders were not involved in the drafting of the Essential Norms, and were hesitant initially to embrace what essentially is a creation of the bishops. As one bishop noted, "If I were a Religious Superior . . . I would feel that our independence has been trampled to some extent, and it has been." Given the vital role of many religious orders in the education of children, it is crucial that the orders follow through on their commitment to apply and follow the Essential Norms.

This is particularly important given that a lack of communication between the religious orders and the dioceses contributed to the problem. There

123

often has been an uneasy relationship between the religious order clergy and the diocesan clergy. Some religious order priests with a history of abuse were sent to various dioceses without disclosure to the dioceses of that history and thereby were enabled to continue to offend. There also was a lack of clarity regarding the responsibilities of a bishop when faced with an accusation concerning a member of a religious order who resides in or works in the bishop's diocese. Then, too, many religious order priests work abroad and therefore are not under the authority of any U.S. bishop. It is the understanding of the Review Board that such a religious priest is subject to the Essential Norms, and that his superior, located in the United States, is responsible for enforcing the Essential Norms. Cooperation among the bishops and religious superiors is critical to ensure that lines of authority and responsibility are clear.[47]

In establishing better communication and clearer lines of authority in this area, the Review Board believes it is important to respect the historical independence of the orders. As one bishop noted, historically, the orders have risen up as "reform movements" when the "bishop and the local Church have become somewhat lax." The orders thus can represent a useful check on the exercise of authority by the

---

[47]   Just as there is concern about U.S. priests engaged in ministry abroad, there is also concern about the large number of foreign-born or foreign-trained priests engaged in ministry in the United States. Bishops and other Church leaders must ensure that these priests also are screened and are given a proper formation and education for chaste celibacy.

bishops. One traditional role of the religious orders, he added, is "to correct the bishop," and to call for greater accountability on his part. The orders, however, did not fulfill their traditional role in relation to the secular clergy in the context of the current crisis; to the contrary, they themselves were plagued by many of the same problems and exacerbated the situation by the same inaction.

### 8.    Episcopal Accountability.

The Review Board found that the failure of bishops to hold themselves accountable for their decisions and to make use of governance structures combined to exacerbate the problem. It would not have been possible for numerous predator priests to continue abusing children even after Church leaders became aware of the abuse were it not for the fact that their bishops effectively lacked accountability. Today, almost two years after the promulgation of the Charter and the Essential Norms, several hundred priests have been removed from ministry, but few bishops have left the episcopacy.

In particular, there appears to have been a general lack of accountability for bishops for the reassignment of priests known to have engaged in the sexual abuse of minors. Perhaps this is because, as one priest put it, "Bishops are not used to explaining their decisions." Such reassignments, which have become public as a result of lawsuits and criminal investigations, seem to have been made by bishops in

125

the belief that they were answerable to no one in the process. This lack of account-ability is one of the causes of the current crisis.

As a matter of Church doctrine, the authority of bishops has its source in the Holy Spirit. As the successors of the apostles, bishops exercise a divinely-given authority. It in no way diminishes this authority to require that bishops must be accountable -- to the Holy Father, to other bishops, and to the Catholic faithful. As stated in the Roman Pontifical in the Homily for the Rite of Ordination of a Bishop, "The title of Bishop is one of service, not of honor, and therefore a Bishop should strive to benefit others rather than to lord it over them. Such is the precept of the Master."

The concept of servant-leadership, and its application to Bishops, was made clear by the Holy Father in November 2003 in his post-synodal Apostolic Exhortation, *Pastores Gregis*, in which he wrote, "All that was said in the Synod Hall about the image of the washing of feet, and the connection made in that context between the figure of the servant and that of the shepherd, helps us to understand that the episcopacy is truly an honour when it is a form of service." (*Pastores Gregis* ¶ 43.) The exercise of authority without accountability is not servant-leadership; it is tyranny. Again, in *Pastores Gregis*, the Holy Father writes, "A lived ecclesial communion will lead the Bishop to a pastoral style which is ever more open to collaboration with all. There is a type of reciprocal interplay between what a Bishop

126

is called to decide with personal responsibility for the good of the Church entrusted to his care and the contribution that the faithful can offer him through consultative bodies . . . ." (*Pastores Gregis* ¶ 44.)

By law and tradition, there are many ways in which other members of the clergy and the laity can help a bishop in his service as leader. These include the authority of the metropolitan archbishop over suffragan bishops, the authority of diocesan councils established by the Code of Canon Law, and the practice of "fraternal correction." As discussed below, however, these governance mechanisms were all but ignored by certain bishops.

### a.    The Selection and Assignment of Bishops.

Many witnesses believe that the crisis has made manifest the need to scrutinize the process for the selection of bishops. Many have expressed concern that the pool of available bishops has been limited too narrowly to those priests who have held positions at the Vatican, in seminaries, and within the diocesan hierarchy. The process needs greater lay involvement, both in putting forth the names of priests who might be considered for the episcopacy and in vetting those who have been put forward, to ensure that a wide net is cast when selecting bishops.

For example, some bishops had had little experience as parish pastors, and therefore may have lacked the ability to understand and relate to the problems and concerns of the laity. Others, who relied on a management mindset rather than a pastoral mindset, were too willing to allow the administrative demands of their dioceses to preempt the human demands of their parishioners.

Because bishops often moved from one diocese to another, there often was insufficient institutional memory within a diocese, at least with respect to individual priests. A new bishop often received little or no information from the prior bishop or his staff about problem priests. Individuals who would have known the identity of these priests (for example, the vicar general) frequently had moved on to new positions. Accordingly, there were many instances where allegations about a particular priest made during the tenure of one bishop never were disclosed to his successor, who then was left to resolve issues with respect to a problem priest on the basis of the most recent allegation only.

Finally, as noted elsewhere in this Report, a "don't-rock-the-boat" attitude prevailed among the bishops for too long. According to many people interviewed by the Board, outspoken priests rarely were selected to be bishops, and the outspoken bishops rarely were selected as archbishops and cardinals. The predictable result was that priests and bishops did not speak out when that is exactly what the situation demanded. Many witnesses believe that the crisis has made manifest a need to open up the type of priests who are chosen as bishops by the Holy See and to reduce the movement of bishops from diocese to diocese to ensure that the bishop develops and maintains strong ties to the local clergy and laity.

Many priests and laity believe that greater lay consultation in the selection of bishops and other aspects of Church governance is required to avoid these problems. The laity largely have been excluded from matters of Church governance in the United States, although fortunately under the Charter they have been asked to play a vital role in reviewing allegations of abuse and restoring trust. Greater involvement of the laity in Church governance might well have lessened both the extent of the current crisis and the magnitude of the laity's negative response to it. In addition, greater involvement by the laity in the selection of bishops could help to ensure that future bishops are pastors, prophets, and men of honor and not mere management functionaries.

### b. Diocesan and Presbyteral Councils.

The bishops failed to make effective use of the accountability mechanisms already built into the Church's structure by Church law through the diocesan councils, and those councils failed to assert themselves. Every diocese is to have a pastoral council which "investigates, considers and proposes practical conclusions about those things which pertain to pastoral works in the diocese." (Canon 511.) Members of this council are to be "designated in a manner determined by the diocesan bishop." (Canon 512 § 1.) Although the role of these councils is consultative only, and they are required to meet only once a year, the Review Board believes

129

they could and should have been more involved in addressing issues of sexual abuse of minors by members of the clergy.

In addition, every diocese should have a presbyteral council (consisting of some priests elected by their fellow priests and others selected by the bishop), whereby priests can make their concerns known to the bishop and assist the bishop in promoting the pastoral welfare of the people of the diocese. (Canons 495, 497.) The utility of these councils will depend upon whether the bishops use them, whether the councils speak frankly, and whether the bishops follow their advice. Obviously, at least with respect to the problem of the sexual abuse of minors by members of the clergy, these councils did not exercise sufficient influence to prevent or mitigate the current crisis.

We cannot accept that the universal law of the Church establishes such councils only to be window-dressing. We know, from the many parish priests that we have spoken to, that the diocesan clergy frequently know or intuit when one of their own has a serious problem – the colleague who never comes to class reunions, who has no contact with his fellow priests, who has visible problems with drugs or alcohol, who establishes age-inappropriate friendships. While the laity of a diocese might not have been as aware as the clergy of these individual problems, they certainly could have given the bishop solid advice on priorities – namely, that protecting their children was more important than the right to ministry of a priest with a history of child sexual abuse. If the bishops had honestly used their diocesan pastoral councils and presbyteral councils to discuss the issue of priests who sexually abused young people, the advice they would have heard well may have prevented the current crisis.

Every diocese also is to have a diocesan finance council, with members appointed by the diocesan bishop. (Canon 492.) Church law requires that this finance council approve all acts of "extraordinary administration" by the diocese. (Canon 1277.) Acts of extraordinary administration are defined as acts that "do not occur regularly and routinely." Certainly the payment of large sums of money to the victims of priest-abusers is not a routine occurrence. Canon law mandates that such payments require review and approval by the diocesan finance council. Yet, to the knowledge of the Review Board, not all dioceses were honoring this requirement.[48] The Board believes that if canon law had been followed in this regard, the crisis would not have grown to its current proportions, because the diocesan practices and underlying conduct that led to such large payments long ago would have been questioned.

---

[48]  As has been publicly reported, the former Archbishop of Milwaukee settled a charge relating to a relationship with an adult male by paying the individual $450,000 out of Church funds. The Archbishop would have been required to seek permission for the payment if it had been $50,000 more. Clearly, a bishop should not be allowed to make such a large payment, whether on behalf of himself or priests in his diocese, with no oversight.

Another body that must review an act of extraordinary administration, such as a large financial settlement for diocesan liability for clergy abuse of young people, is the college of consultors. (Canon 1277.) This is a group of six to twelve priests chosen by the diocesan bishop from among the members of the diocesan priests' council. While a diocesan bishop could choose from the priests' council as consultors only those priests who he knows will tell him what he wants to hear, that would be contrary to the spirit of the law. Canon 127, which establishes the legal elements for "consent" and "advice" when they are required by the law, speaks of the "sincere opinion" of those whose advice or consent is required. It is not meant to be a rubber-stamp process. Greater involvement by the college of consultors would have helped bishops respond to allegations of sexual abuse of minors by clergy more appropriately.

Bishops need not fear the active participation of faithful Catholics, whether they be clergy or laity, when they function in these councils required by the Church's own law. Pope John Paul II writes in *Pastores Gregis*:

> If communion expresses the church's essence, then it is normal that
> the spirituality of communion will tend to manifest itself in both the
> personal and community spheres, awakening ever new forms of
> participation and shared responsibility in the faithful of every cate-
> gory. Consequently, the Bishop will make every effort to develop,
> within his particular Church, structures of communion and participa-
> tion which makes it possible to listen to the Spirit who lives and
> speaks in the faithful, in order to guide them in carrying out whatever
> the same Spirit suggests for the true good of the Church.

(*Pastores Gregis* ¶ 44.) Bishops need to learn to trust these councils of laity and clergy and learn "to listen to the Spirit who lives and speaks" in them. Ignoring these bodies was a significant factor in the cause of the current crisis.

In sum, the People of God are both clergy and laity. They both have a role. Priests and bishops must learn to trust the laity and not fear their participation in the life of the Church. The lay faithful must learn to exercise their roles within the structure of the Church. The clergy, especially the bishops, teach the faith authoritatively. Lay people do not. The clergy exercise the full power of governance. Lay people do not. But turning to the laity and relying on the participation of the laity does not subvert this structure and does not diminish the authority of the bishops. Already in the structure of the Church there is a requirement for bishops to rely on the advice, and sometimes even the approval, of consultative bodies, such as the diocesan pastoral council or the diocesan finance council. If the laity demand that these bodies truly function – staffed with talented, faithful, independent laypersons giving the bishops honest advice – they are only asking that the bishops follow the law of the Church.

### c. The Roles of the Metropolitan and the Conference.

By tradition and by Church law, the metropolitan, an archbishop at the head of an ecclesiastical province (a geographic grouping of dioceses), is charged with exercising some degree of authority over the bishops within his province.

133

Canonically, a metropolitan has certain oversight authority with respect to the other bishops, known as "suffragan" bishops, in his province. Several witnesses with whom we spoke believe that the historical authority of the metropolitan has waned, and needs to be reinvigorated. The Holy Father also urged recently that the bishops "restore vitality" to this "ancient institution." (*Pastores Gregis* ¶ 62.) As one bishop told the Board, an effective metropolitan should intervene with a "recalcitrant bishop" in his area and "take it to the Congregations of Bishops in Rome." Of course, when the "recalcitrant bishop" is himself a metropolitan, such a hierarchy is of limited utility. In such a situation, however, the suffragan bishops should have the courage to raise their concerns with the metropolitan and with other bishops.

As the authority of the metropolitans tended to wane during the last three decades of the twentieth century, the prominence, if not authority, of the national conference of bishops grew. The U.S. Conference of Catholic Bishops, however, exercises no power over its bishop members. As one bishop said of the Conference, "They have zero authority over the local bishop." Thus, although the Conference promulgated guidelines for dealing with allegations of sexual abuse of minors by clergy in 1992, individual bishops were under no obligation to follow the guidelines, and some did not. The Conference also considered authorizing a study to look at the problem of clerical sexual abuse of minors in the late 1980s and again in the early 1990s, but too few bishops voted to proceed and the project was shelved.

Even though the Conference could not have exercised binding authority over bishops, it could have served as a clearinghouse for information and a resource for the formulation of a coherent, appropriate response by the United States dioceses to the problem of sexual abuse of minors by members of the U.S. clergy. Because dioceses did not share information with other dioceses about incidents of alleged abuse, however, many bishops failed to realize that the problem was national in scope and not limited to certain dioceses. As a result, there was insufficient communication between dioceses and orders, both with respect to specific priests and with respect to evolving best practices for responding to allegations of sexual abuse.

This experience has led some witnesses with whom the Review Board met to question whether more power should not be given to the national conferences. There are, however, strong arguments against investing national conferences with greater power. As a matter of creed, the Catholic Church is universal. There is, institutionally, no "Church of the United States," or "Church of China." There is only "one holy Catholic Apostolic Church." Some fear that giving additional authority to national conferences would widen rifts between nations and tend to weaken the universality of the Church. Furthermore, as Pope John Paul II has emphasized, conferences must avoid "an excessively bureaucratic development of offices and commissions" and bishops must keep in mind that conferences "exist to

135

be of help to the Bishops and not to substitute for them." (*Pastores Gregis* ¶ 63; *cf.* Pope John Paul II, Motu Proprio, *Apostulos Suos* 653 (1998).)

The Review Board believes nonetheless that the bishops must devise ways to make greater use of the Conference to ensure that dioceses learn from each other, and that recalcitrant bishops are not allowed to expose the Church to risks such as those that precipitated the current crisis. Ultimately, of course, discipline of bishops who do not act in accordance with the requirements of canon law is a matter for the Apostolic See. But the Vatican cannot act on such matters if they are left to languish beyond its field of vision.

Some witnesses suggested that dioceses can perform a much more important job of monitoring other dioceses in a way that involves neither a reinvigoration of the authority of the metropolitan nor an expansion of the authority of the Conference. Specifically, just as universities and colleges undergo an accreditation process whereby professionals from other institutions are invited to visit and examine them on a regular basis, it is possible that a similar process could be developed within the present strictures of canon law to bring greater oversight to the performance of bishops. A visitation of the diocese, conducted by one or two bishops from another diocese as well as competent priests and lay people from other dioceses, could be undertaken in conjunction with the quinquennial *ad limina* visit to the Apostolic See that every bishop undertakes. Although Vatican oversight would be

136

needed for such a process, the diocesan *ad limina* visitation could consist of a review of books and records, policies such as the sexual abuse policy, and discussions with priests and selected laity from the diocese.

There is ample precedent for such an outside review in the practices of the religious orders. Although these diocesan *ad limina* visitations would be voluntarily entered into, the Review Board believes that a bishop who wished to be responsive to his priests and people would welcome the fresh look that only an outside perspective can bring. Certainly, by agreeing to such a review the bishop would send a signal to other bishops and to the faithful in his diocese that he intends to lead with transparency and accountability.

### d.    Fraternal Correction.

It is perhaps understandable that bishops and priests may be reluctant to tell others that they are acting wrongly, but it is their responsibility to do so. The history of the Church is replete with examples of bishops properly taking other bishops to task, beginning with Paul's remonstrance to Peter at Antioch. (Galatians 2:11.) For some reason, however, confronted with the problem of sexual abuse of minors by clergy, such instances of fraternal correction – a private process in which brother bishops may offer criticism of each other – have been the exception, not the rule.

Fraternal correction is a natural outgrowth of the collegiality of the bishops and it should be, as Pope John Paul II says in *Pastores Gregis* (¶ 8), based upon "the Bishops' concern for the other particular churches [*i.e.*, dioceses]." As a member of the college of bishops, no bishop is ever alone. He is "always and continuously united with his brothers in the episcopate." (*Id.*) From this union flows at least a moral responsibility to correct errant brother bishops. For example, it was reported to the Review Board that the response of one bishop to the suggested adoption of the Five Principles in 1992 was: "No one is going to tell me how to run my diocese." We do not know what the reaction of his fellow bishops was to this statement, but we hope that, should such a statement be made today, the other bishops would correct such myopia by telling the bishop that no one, not even a bishop, has the right to risk the well-being of youngsters entrusted to his care; nor does he have the right to risk the good name of his fellow bishops and the entire Church in the United States by his intransigence.[49]

---

[49] In this regard, the Board notes that although the bishops in general demonstrated support for the work of the Board and the John Jay College survey, the vicar general for the Diocese of Lincoln (Nebraska) wrote a letter indicating that the Most Reverend Fabian Bruskewitz, Bishop of Lincoln, would not cooperate with the efforts of either the Board or John Jay College. Specifically, the letter stated that Bishop Bruskewitz "does not recognize any jurisdiction claimed over him or his pastoral activity by the 'National Review Board'" and that he "is prepared to take any appropriate and suitable measures necessary, including legal action, were that Board, your institution, or the United States Conference of Catholic Bishops to attempt to coerce him by

(continued...)

The Review Board was surprised and distressed to hear bishops acknowledging that "there's none of this networking [among bishops] going on that should be going on," and urging that ways be found to help bishops "bring pressure on the brother bishops." As one individual told the Board, "Only one, or very, very few members of [the Conference] are willing to get up, even in the executive session, and say, 'Your Excellency, Your Eminence, this is wrong.'" This absence of fraternal correction compounded the lack of episcopal accountability and further fueled the current crisis.

## V.  RECOMMENDATIONS.

The Charter and Essential Norms have placed the Catholic Church in the United States on a course to ensure the safety of its children and young people and to recover the confidence of the laity that so badly has been shaken by the current crisis. The Review Board believes, however, that additional measures are necessary to hasten that recovery and ensure that it is complete.

### A.  Further Study and Analysis.

- The bishops and religious ordinaries should continue to support the undertaking of a comprehensive scientific study relating to the causes and context of sexual abuse in the Church

---

[49]  (...continued)
adverse publicity, the threat of such, or other similar actions."

and in society. In Article 16 of the Charter, the bishops pledged their willingness to cooperate in such research "with other churches and ecclesial communities, other religious bodies, institutions of learning, and other interested organizations." The problem of sexual abuse of minors is a societal problem, and the Church can take the lead in addressing the problem throughout society.[50]

- The bishops should agree to ongoing diocesan audits to ensure compliance with the Charter and the Essential Norms.

- There should be a periodic review of the effectiveness and fairness of the zero-tolerance policy to ensure the application of individualized justice.

**B.     Enhanced Screening, Formation, and Oversight.**

- Bishops and seminary leaders must ensure that each candidate is a mature, psychologically well-adjusted individual, with an unequivocal commitment to a life of service to the Church and her people, and a clear understanding of the challenges of the priesthood, including celibacy, before admission into the seminary. A bishop must get to know each potential candidate and exercise good judgment in determining whether the candidate is suitable for the priesthood. Candidates should be thoroughly vetted through all appropriate methods.

---

[50]    The next step for the bishops and the Board is to commission a broad-based and multi-year study of the epidemic of abuse that the John Jay College study describes. It is hoped that such a study will identify the interactive causal factors in a systematic, epidemiological (host/victim-agent/predator-environment/culture) fashion. Such a study will enable the Church to develop additional policies for the protection of children and also will bring light to the factors that lead to child abuse in society at large and the steps that can be taken to protect children from the physical and psychological trauma of sexual abuse in the future.

140

- Seminaries must provide better preparation for the challenges of living a celibate life in today's culture.

- Seminaries must institute rigorous procedures for continually evaluating the suitability of those admitted to study for the priesthood, as well as mechanisms (including expulsion) for addressing problems identified in the evaluation process.

- Seminaries themselves must be more rigorously evaluated. The upcoming Apostolic Visitation should be conducted by independent, knowledgeable individuals who can provide an honest, informed, and unbiased evaluation. It must examine both the curriculum and the formation program. To the extent that institutions operating certain seminaries are not providing adequate oversight, the seminaries should be placed under different authority.

- A healthy priest is connected to God, connected to his bishop or religious superior, connected to his fellow priests, and connected to the People of God. Accordingly, there must be ongoing intellectual, spiritual, and psychological formation and monitoring of priests after ordination. Priests should be encouraged to participate in fellowship groups with other priests, to form close, healthy relationships with priests and with laity, and to maintain an active prayer life.

- Bishops must meet frequently with their priests to monitor their morale and emotional well-being. A bishop must know his priests.

- Each bishop should meet annually with the religious superior for any non-diocesan priests who are resident in his diocese to ensure that the religious superior takes responsibility for monitoring the non-diocesan priests engaged in ministry in the diocese.

C. **Increased Sensitivity and Effectiveness in Responding to Allegations of Abuse.**

- Seeing to the welfare of victims of abuse must be the primary duty of the Church when confronted with evidence of abuse. Dioceses must ensure that victims of clergy sexual abuse are encouraged to come forward and are treated with respect, dignity, and compassion.

- Bishops and Church leaders must recognize both the criminal and the sinful nature of the sexual abuse of minors by members of the clergy. Bishops must respond vigorously to all allegations of abuse, maintain accurate records of such allegations and the responses thereto, and openly exchange information with other dioceses about such allegations.

- All bishops and leaders of religious orders should meet with victims and their families to obtain a better understanding of the harm caused by the sexual abuse of minors by clergy. Bishops and leaders of religious orders must be personally involved in this issue and not delegate a matter of such importance to others.

- In assessing individual cases in order to determine whether the priest engaged in an act of sexual abuse of a minor and therefore must be removed from ministry, bishops and other Church leaders should honor the rights of accused priests and consult with their lay review boards, so that together they might strive for individualized justice in light of their developing experience and expertise.

- Dioceses and religious orders should re-examine their litigation strategies to ensure that a pastoral response takes precedence over legal tactics. Dioceses should eschew litigation when possible and earnestly pursue other avenues of resolving allegations of abuse.

- In seeking therapeutic options for priests who have engaged in sexual abuse of minors, the dioceses should use only well-qualified treatment centers that specialize in treating sexual disorders and that are able and willing to evaluate patient outcomes in a disinterested professional fashion.

- The Church should make use of national or regional canonical tribunals in the United States to consider cases for laicization under the Charter in order to ensure that experienced individuals hear and decide these cases and that they are decided in a consistent fashion. Bishops should ensure that the appropriate authorities at the Vatican are provided with a comprehensive and complete file to review when determining whether to laicize a priest.

## D. Greater Accountability of Bishops and Other Church Leaders.

- The process for selecting bishops should include meaningful lay consultation.

- The bishops should trust and learn to make greater use of those consultative and deliberative bodies established by canon law to assist them in the pastoral care and governance of their dioceses. These bodies should be filled with faithful laypersons and priests who are talented, responsible, and dedicated to the Church, but who are also capable of offering, and who are expected to offer, truly independent counsel to the bishop.

- The Church should consider restoring and strengthening the role of the metropolitan archbishop in overseeing suffragan bishops and should consider steps to enable the national conferences to serve as information clearinghouses and to provide enhanced information flow among dioceses about critical issues facing the Church.

- The bishops should be more willing to engage in fraternal correction and should appeal to the Vatican to intervene if a particular bishop appears unable or unwilling to act in the best interests of the entire Church.

- An audit team through the Office of Child and Youth Protection should review the handling of abuse allegations by individual dioceses and orders. The audit team should publish its findings in a report so that the laity will be apprised of the results.

### E.    Improved Interaction with Civil Authorities.

- Dioceses and orders should report all allegations of sexual abuse to the civil authorities, regardless of the circumstances, or the age or perceived credibility of the accuser.

- Dioceses and orders should endeavor to resolve civil claims and government investigations on reasonable terms and in a manner that minimizes the potential for intrusion of civil authorities into the governance of Church matters.

### F.    Meaningful Participation by the Christian Faithful in the Church.

- The bishops and other Church leaders must listen to and be responsive to the concerns of the laity. To accomplish this, the hierarchy must act with less secrecy, more transparency, and a greater openness to the gifts that all members of the Church bring to her.

Finally, it has been observed that the current crisis at heart is one of faith and morality. Accordingly, the Review Board believes that, ultimately, the resolution of the crisis will require an abiding faith and commitment to morality for all members of the Church.

# CODA

In making public this report and recognizing the stain that it exposes on the Church that we love, we can but recall the Old Testament words of the psalmist who taught that while hidden guilt festers, honest admission of guilt heals:

> As long as I kept silent,
> My bones wasted away;
> I groaned all the day . . .
> Then I declared my sin to you;
> my guilt I did not hide.
> I said, "I confess my faults to the Lord,"
> and you took away the guilt of my sin.

(Psalm 32.)

It is with that faith in the merciful powers of the Almighty that we members of the National Review Board offer the candid judgments we have been asked to give. How, one may ask, can any forgiveness, much less renewal, emerge from such a sordid history of misdeeds? We are inspired, as always, by the example of Jesus, who two thousand years ago founded this Church and who during his life on earth once instructed his disciples: "For human beings this is impossible, but for God all things are possible."

**Appendix To The Report on the Crisis in the
Catholic Church in the United States.**

**National Review Board
for the Protection of Children and Young People**

**List of Interviews**

Between December 2002 and January 2004, the Review Board's

Research Committee conducted sixty separate interviews with more than eighty-five

individuals. All but a few of the interviews were conducted in person; the remaining

interviews were conducted via teleconference. All individuals listed below partici-

pated in formal interviews with the Board. In addition, the Review Board consulted

numerous other individuals on a more informal basis.

**Archibald,** Susan
*President, The Linkup - Survivors of Clergy Abuse*

**Arinze,** Francis Cardinal
*Prefect of Divine Worship and the Discipline of the Sacraments, Roman Curia,
The Vatican*

**Bendall,** James, Esq.
*Counsel, Roman Catholic Faithful*

**Berlin,** Fred, M.D.
*Psychiatrist, Associate Professor, Johns Hopkins School of Medicine*

**Berry,** Jason
*Author*

**Bevilacqua,** Anthony Cardinal
*Archbishop Emeritus of Philadelphia*

**Brady,** Steven
*President, Roman Catholic Faithful*

**Byrne,** Monsignor Harry J.
*Retired Pastor; Representative of Retired Priests, Priests' Council for Archdiocese of New York*

**Byron,** Reverend William J., S.J.
*Former Pastor, Holy Trinity Church, Washington, D.C.; President Loyola University of New Orleans; Author*

**Chopko,** Mark, Esq.
*General Counsel, United States Conference of Catholic Bishops*

**Cimbolic,** Professor Peter, Ph.D.
*Psychotherapist; Provost and Vice President for Academic Affairs, Bellarmine University*

**Clergy Misconduct Oversight Board, Selected Members, Archdiocese of Los Angeles**
Judi Arnold
The Honorable Richard P. Byrne
Reverend Jarlath Cunnane, V.F.
Nanette de Fuentes, Ph.D.
Sister Diane Donoghue
Adrienne Cedro-Hament
Yvonne Mariajimenez
Terry Seidler
George K. Takahashi

**Clergy Review Board, Selected Members, Archdiocese of St. Paul-Minneapolis**
Reverend Michael Byron
Dr. David Drees
Edward Fox, Esq.

**Clohessy,** David
*Director, Survivors Network of Those Abused By Priests (SNAP)*

**Connors,** Reverend Canice, OFM Conv.
*Former President, Conference of Major Superiors of Men; Former Executive Director, St. Luke's Institute*

**Cox,** Monsignor Craig A.
*Vicar for Clergy for the Archdiocese of Los Angeles*

**Cozzens,** Reverend Donald B.
*Priest of the Diocese of Cleveland; Pastoral Psychologist; Author*

**D'Arcy,** The Most Reverend John M.
*Bishop of Fort Wayne-South Bend, Indiana*

**Dolan,** The Most Reverend Timothy
*Archbishop of Milwaukee*

**Doyle,** Reverend Thomas P., O.P.
*Priest; Canon Lawyer; Major, United States Air Force*

**Egan,** Edward Cardinal
*Archbishop of New York*

**Farrell,** Sister Carolyn, B.V.M.
*Director of the Ann Ida Gannon, B.V.M., Center for Women and Leadership*

**Flynn,** The Most Reverend Harry J.
*Archbishop of St. Paul-Minneapolis*

**George,** Francis Cardinal, O.M.I.
*Archbishop of Chicago*

**Greeley,** Reverend Andrew M.
*Priest of the Archdiocese of Chicago; Author; Professor of Sociology, Loyola University of Chicago*

**Happel,** Reverend Stephen P.
*Former Dean, School of Religious Studies, The Catholic University of America; Sociologist*

**Hodgman,** William W., Esq.
*Assistant District Attorney, City of Los Angeles*

**Hoge,** Professor Dean, Ph.D.
*Professor of Sociology, The Catholic University of America*

**Hynes,** The Honorable Charles J.
*District Attorney of Kings County, New York*

**Hurley,** The Most Reverend Walter A.
*Auxiliary Bishop of Detroit*

**Karabin,** Joseph
*Inactive Priest of the Diocese of Pittsburgh*

**Keating,** Reverend Timothy G., SM
*Executive Director, Conference of Major Superiors of Men*

**Keeler,** William Cardinal
*Archbishop of Baltimore*

**Kennedy,** Eugene C., Ph.D.
*Former Priest; Author; Psychologist*

**Kinney,** The Most Reverend John F.
*Bishop of St. Cloud, Minnesota*

**Lasch,** Monsignor Kevin
*Pastor, St. Joseph's Church, Mendham, New Jersey*

**Law,** Bernard Cardinal
*Archbishop Emeritus of Boston*

**Lennon,** The Most Reverend Richard
*Auxiliary Bishop of Boston*

**Loomis,** Monsignor Richard A.
*Former Vicar for Clergy for the Archdiocese of Los Angeles*

**Lopez Trujillo,** Alfonso Cardinal
*President of the Pontifical Council for the Family, Roman Curia, The Vatican*

**Lori,** The Most Reverend William
*Bishop of Bridgeport*

**Lothstein,** Leslie, Ph.D.
*Director, Clinical Psychology Services, The Institute of Living*

**Mahony,** Roger Cardinal
*Archbishop of Los Angeles*

**Maida,** Adam Cardinal
*Archbishop of Detroit*

**Maniscalco,** Monsignor Francis
*Director, USCCB Department of Communications*

**Markham,** Sister Donna, O.P.
*Psychologist; Former President, Southdown Institute; Special Assistant to the President, Georgetown University*

**McCarrick,** Theodore Cardinal
*Archbishop of Washington*

**McCloskey,** Heidi, R.N.
*Former Admissions Director of the Professionals' Program, The Institute of Living*

**McCormack,** The Most Reverend John B.
*Bishop of Manchester (New Hampshire)*

**McKenna,** Reverend Kevin
*Priest of the Diocese of Rochester; Canon Lawyer*

**Mixner,** David
*President, DMB & Associates; Political Strategist and Gay-rights Activist*

**Mulkerrin,** Sister Catherine, CSJ
*Former Assistant to the Delegate for Priestly Personnel, Archdiocese of Boston*

**Murphy,** Sister Judy, CSJ
*General Counsel, Archdiocese of Los Angeles*

**Newman,** Reverend Jay Scott
*Pastor, St. Mary's Catholic Church, Greenville, South Carolina*

**O'Malley,** The Most Reverend Seán Patrick, O.F.M. Cap.
*Archbishop of Boston*

**Orsy,** Reverend Ladislas, S.J.
*Theologian; Professor of Law, Georgetown University Law Center*

**Pates,** The Most Reverend Richard E.
*Auxiliary Bishop of St. Paul-Minneapolis*

**Podles,** Leon, Ph.D.
*Contributing Editor, Touchstone Magazine; Author*

**Ratzinger,** Joseph Cardinal
*Prefect of Congregation for the Doctrine of the Faith, Roman Curia, The Vatican*

**Reese,** Reverend Thomas J., S.J.
*Editor of America Magazine*

**Rossetti,** Reverend Stephen J., Ph.D.
*Priest of Diocese of Syracuse; Psychologist; Author; President, St. Luke Institute*

**Schiltz,** Professor Patrick
*Professor, University of St. Thomas Law Center; Canon Lawyer*

**Schwartz,** Harold I., M.D.
*Psychiatrist-In-Chief, The Institute of Living*

**Seminarians** at the North American Pontifical College

**Seminarians** at St. Mary's Seminary, Archdiocese of Baltimore

**Serrano,** Mark
*Member of the Board, Survivors Network of those Abuse by Priests (SNAP)*

**Sheehan,** Archbishop Michael J.
*Archbishop of Santa Fe; Former Apostolic Administrator, Diocese of Phoenix*

**Silva,** Reverend Robert
*President, National Federation of Priests' Councils*

**Sipe,** A.W. Richard
*Former Priest; Author*

**Stafford,** James Cardinal
*Major Penitentiary of Apostolic Penitentiary, Roman Curia, The Vatican; Former Archbishop of Denver*

**Talbot,** The Honorable Michael J.
*Chairperson of the Archdiocesan Review Board, Archdiocese of Detroit*

**Vadakin,** Monsignor Royale
*Vicar General, Archdiocese of Los Angeles*

**Weakland,** The Most Reverend Rembert, O.S.B.
*Archbishop Emeritus of Milwaukee*

**Weigel,** George
*Senior Fellow, Ethics and Public Policy Center; Author*

**White,** Reverend Mark
*Associate Pastor, St. Raphael's Catholic Church, Rockville, Maryland*

**Witherup,** Reverend Ronald D., SS
*President, Conference of Major Superiors of Men*

**Youniss,** Professor James
*Professor of Psychology, The Catholic University of America; Author*

***Zullo,*** Br. James R., Ph.D.
*Psychologist; Senior Chaplain, Loyola University of Chicago*

\*　　\*　　\*

The Review Board notes that all witnesses participated in the Board's interviews voluntarily and paid for their own expenses associated with the interview. The Board is grateful for their assistance.